SHELLCRAFT

RADNOR, PENNSYLVANIA

Copyright © 1974 by Cleo M. Stephens
First Edition
All rights reserved
Published in Radnor, Pa., by Chilton Book Company
and simultaneously in Ontario, Canada,
by Thomas Nelson & Sons, Ltd.
Photographs by Cleo M. Stephens
Designed by Warren Infield
Manufactured in the United States of America

Library of Congress Cataloging in Publication Data

Stephens, Cleo.
   Shellcraft.

   Bibliography: p.
   1. Shellcraft.   I. Title.
TT862.S73   1974   745.55   74-1101
ISBN 0-8019-5886-5
ISBN 0-8019-5885-7 (pbk.)

FOR MELANIE AND PAULA
WHO LOVE THE SEA AND THE SHELLING

Acknowledgments

My thanks go to all the great craft and collecting books, especially those listed in the reference section; to The Florida Supply House, for filling orders for shells so promptly; to The Shell Factory, for the helpful cooperation of its people; to the managers of the Sanibel and Ft. Myers Shell Shows, for their help; to Margaret Fishback, who joined me in my first shell art work; to Pam Jones, whose lovely hands are subjects in several of the how-to pictures; to Margaret Elgersman, who cheerfully permitted me to photograph her shell art work; to the Mao family, who also permitted the photographing of their shell art; to Larry and Leona Elton and Arthur and Phillis Anderson, whose interest was a constant morale booster, and to all those other great people, too numerous to mention, whose interest in the project was unflagging.

Particularly do my thanks go to my husband, Ray, and my daughters, Darlene and Shirley, whose love and confidence in my ability sustain me in all my many projects.

Contents

List of Illustrations

X

Color Plates

Introduction

An author cannot share the experience of writing novels, for these write themselves—at least mine have. Incidents occur out of thin air, and ghost-like characters materialize from nowhere. The pencil (I write my first draft in longhand) pushes faster and faster, forced on by the writer's avid desire to find out what's going to happen next.

But a nonfiction book, especially one that entails the creation of beautiful artwork, is an altogether different situation; unlike the novel with its easy, racing story plot, a nonfiction work makes me do the work. It drives me, relentless in its intensity, to meticulously work out the smallest detail; every step of every piece must fall precisely into place to make a complete whole.

I must experience most of the things I write about rather than merely research them. For an article on survival, I found it necessary to put myself into a position where I had to learn survival techniques; in doing an article on a bottomless, water-filled cave where scuba divers had died, I donned wet suit and scuba gear and learned to dive in that frightening place. How else could I know the feeling of those divers who swam down there, lost in the black depths, until their air gave out?

For an article on sea horses, we floated the saltwater bays. Draped over the edge of the canoe, we peered down through the crystal clear water to watch the fascinating life of those little creatures among the sea grasses and on the white sand. Studying those we had in our aquarium was not enough, we had to see them in their natural habitat as well. Only thus could we feel that we could speak with authority. I cannot believe a writer can do this by merely reading about someone else's experiences.

And so it was with *Shellcraft*. I had previously made many pieces of shell art, and as an amateur archeologist, I had studied a great deal about ancient people's use of shells for both practical and ornamental purposes, but not until starting the actual writing and photographing of this book did I know the immensely satisfying joys the craft has to offer. I wanted to make every item I wrote about, and except for a very few, I did just that. Luckily my understanding husband, Ray, took over the making of shadow boxes—no little job when it came to forming shadow boxes for the old oval frames. I also seem to remember bacon and egg meals and an occasional chicken dinner (catered by Col. Sanders) appearing when I had been lost all morning in the darkroom.

In some instances, photographing for the book was real labor. The photos were tricky, especially those behind glass; lighting and reflections caused trouble, and close-ups and angles were a problem. It was often necessary to spend many long, tiring hours and days in the darkroom dodging out unwanted objects that had somehow gotten into the picture and burning in those I was actually featuring.

The wealth of art grew and grew, like the rice pot output of the old fable, until the hutch and the breakfast bar were loaded and all the available wall space was covered. Finally, the dining table disappeared under a load, and from then on all our meals were consumed in the kitchen.

We had collected vast numbers of the shells we would need, but most of them had been used for a nursing home craft project, so there were times when we were far from the seashore and desperately needed certain shells. At these times I shamelessly scrounged from friends!

Then I managed to get hold of some shell shop catalogs, and the search went on via Uncle Sam's postal department. The discovery that there are actually shell shops where mail orders as small as twenty cents can be placed was a surprise. We have listed these shops in the back of the book.

We have attempted to make *Shellcraft* a thing of fun rather than a study course in conchology or malacology. This study is best left to another type of book and to authors more knowledgeable in this science than we are. For this reason we have used the descriptive terms for shells wherever possible. For instance, lucinas are cup shells and certain clams, that are shaped like a dogwood petal, are called dogwood shells (see Figs. 2.1 and 2.2). One reason we have done this is that shellcraft shops list shells this way in their catalogs, and thus our system should make it easier for you to order the shells you need.

Flowers are described in the *Encyclopaedia Britannica* with such obtuse words as peduncle, pedicel and raceme. But since few of us are botanists, and none of us wants to take time out to look up these words when in the middle of a work session, we have again let the descriptive terms tell the story. Everyone immediately envisions a certain shape when "cluster flowers" is mentioned, and "spray" adequately describes another form.

Writing the text of this book in the "duo" form, "we," was not a mere journalistic gimmick. That best of all husbands, Ray Stephens, who loyally backs me in even my wildest projects, entered wholeheartedly into this one, both aiding and abetting.

And so, dear reader, we leave this introductory chapter, with the Stephens being gradually shoved from house and home by the vast mass of shell art that has accumulated.

Now what to do with all these beautiful, laboriously constructed items! We are swamped, but so much of me has gone into these creations that it would be difficult to give up any of them.

1

Romance of the Sea

There is something about the sea—something intangible, untouchable that permeates the senses. We feel its age subconsciously. It has the majesty and power to draw, hold and awe the soul of man as nothing else can.

Our first meeting with the sea, at whatever age it might come, no matter if that first contact is with the gentle sigh of the reef-protected waters of the Gulf of Mexico, the massive roll of an Atlantic surf, the crashing, giant breakers of California's Pacific coast or the high-ridged rollers of Hawaii's surfing waters, stirs some primitive, forgotten song within us.

In the lapping edge of the waves, the firm sand deteriorates like quick-silver from beneath our feet; our guard is lowered. One moment the sea toys delicately, teasingly at bare feet, and then without warning, it comes down upon us with a tearing, crashing wall of water that grasps us in its tenacious grip and tries to drag us back to the depths from which life once escaped.

And always there is the drawing power of the song of the sea—rising, falling, ever-changing. When we cast aside the mystery and delve into the facts, we realize what is responsible for that song—it is the melody created by the shells as they are tumbled, grated and crushed by the sea. Without the little creatures of the sea there would be no song. The welk and conch and abalone and snail, the clam and scallop and cowrie and all little creatures who so painstakingly formed their homes of lime, fulfill their destiny by adding another note to the song of the sea.

Treasures of the Sea

The sea offers us many treasures. Up through the surf and onto the beach are swept shells so varied and beautiful that as we examine them a new fascination is born. Some people invariably become collectors—beachcombers who roam the sands, losing all sense of time and place. Each drift of shells contains new and exotic species of varying colors; we are driven to wander on and on, searching and collecting not only shells, but many other sea treasures (see Fig. 1.1). We fill hands, then pockets, then hats and finally we graduate to baskets and boxes.

So, now that we have all those shells, what are we going to do with them? Well, since man's desire to accumulate possessions is so deeply ingrained and since it is a part of his nature to use his hands for creative art, why not combine the two and utilize shells for art objects?

Shell Art through the Ages

The use of shells is certainly not new to our generation, or even to our century. From the beginning man has used them for the practical and the esthetic. A large conch or clam, in the hands of ancient man, became a kitchen utensil serving many purposes, from drinking cup to storage container. He used the colorful smaller shells to create objects of beauty and adornment.

Even as far back as in the days of the early Sumerians a great value was put on seashells as material for ornamentation. Shells were even considered worthy of use with precious metals and gems, such as gold, lapis lazuli and other gemstones, in the creation of jewelry and the decoration of fine art treasures. Iridescent mother-of-pearl was also widely used on both small and large objects.

Many shell and gemstone mosaics on other objects have been found in Babylonian excavations. Shells and gemstones were used to make the trimming on large objects, such as the manes of golden lions that decorated royal chariots and the curly wool of lambs. The upright stanchions of a magnificent harp were embellished with red stone, white shell, lapis lazuli and gold. And all of this was done by craftsmen in about the year 3000 B.C.!

We find that the American Indian was no exception; he made use of shells in all the old ways and invented some uses of his own. Even today you may find bells made of shells, pierced and strung on thongs, on the ankles and across the chests of Indian ceremonial dancers. Shells are also used to trim headdresses and clothing. Indians combined beauty and utility when they so laboriously used crude tools to cut and bore the beads and shells that

Fig. 1.1 Treasures other than shells to keep a lookout for when beachcombing. These more unusual items (driftwood, sea whips, starfish) will be used in beach scenes and underwater scenes.

served as money, personal adornment and decoration. In this day of diamond-cutting implements, it is difficult to envision the work that was involved in the intricate carving of shells. Shells were so valued for ornamentation that archeologists have found jewelry made of shells at locations hundreds of miles from the sea.

The amazing thing is that many of the shell objects found are not crude, sketchily made items but were definitely made by skilled craftsmen. Shell jewelry, inlaid with mosaics of turquoise, was made by a desert people called Hohokams, in about the year 1400. A sticky substance deposited on creosote bushes by insects was used to glue the tiny bits of stone in place.

There are probably few countries in the world whose people have not used shells for both practical and ornamental purposes. From torrid Africa to icy Alaska, from India to Iceland, people have prized the lustrous beauty of shells and used them in their works of art. African girls wore, and still wear, cowries strung for headbands, belts, bracelets and anklets; Hawaiians wore, and still wear, leis made of shells.

Some shell art objects of the past are now treasured museum pieces, others are family heirlooms. Perhaps some of the shell art pieces you make will be the treasured possessions of your great-great-grandchildren, for creative art always has been and always will be recognized as the most enduring way both primitive and highly civilized man has ever had of expressing his innermost love of beauty.

The expenditure of hours in the creation of objects of art cannot be called a waste of time, for in them is enthroned the soul of a human being. Not all men have equal talents, of course, but whether that article of art is intricate gold filigree, inlay of shell or precious stone or even a crude wood-carving, the talents that are peculiarly our own have gone into the making of it, and our pride at its completion brings an immense satisfaction.

So we can take a page from the past and create art of lasting value from our shells; there are endless possibilities to test our ingenuity and talent. All we need are a few basic instructions, a few simple materials and some of the shells that are so prolifically strewn on our seashores. And even if we cannot have the good fortune to roam the beaches, there are shops where almost any shells we might need can be purchased. In some cases, these shops have a mail order department and put out catalogs. We have listed some of these in the back of the book.

2

Shells

It is not our intention to go into the field of the conchologist in this book; that field contains subject matter for a volume all its own. Collection for the sake of collection, as the conchologist views it, requires the discussion of the value of certain species of shells, their rarity and the locations in which each individual specimen has been found. For the shell craftsman not all of this is relevant. All he needs to know, for the most part, is where the variety of shells applicable to his needs can be found.

However, this is not to say that a single beautiful shell, displayed on its own attractive stand, should not have a part in shellcraft discussion—it should. And the fact that it was created by a power whose methods are far beyond our comprehension makes it no less a work of art. And too, we must recognize the fact that value does enter into the picture, for when a single shell brings a sum of $1,200—as did the last glory-of-the-sea sold—we sit up and take notice with sheer awe.

So you may go into this shell thing as deeply as you like, it is a matter of choice. You can play at it, simply collecting a few for Aunt Minnie; collect in earnest for displays; make animals and birds; or elevate it to an art form by creating valuable heirlooms.

One can construct a clever little critter or create a decorative wall plaque six feet long, fasten a display of shells to a fish net draped on the wall of the den, or recreate an underwater scene behind glass. Or one may go so deeply into this craft as to carve on shell the face or figure of a person or animal and thus produce a valuable cameo. And if this is not intricate enough, you could try your hand at the mother-of-pearl inlay that was used in the Orient for many thousands of years on jewelry, fans, buttons and jewelry boxes, and even in mosaic designs that decorated temples, furniture and homes.

These skills do not spring into being full-blown but must be tenderly nourished from the birth of the desire through the various, stumbling steps of learning. It is the purpose of this book to help serve as a guide through that labyrinth.

So you love to go shelling, and you want to have a reason to continue shelling—what do you do with all those shells? You can set some of the largest and handsomest around the house in conspicuous spots for decorative pieces; you can give an assortment to Aunt Minnie, who has never had the good fortune to see an ocean; you can give favorite little neighborhood kids some of the more unusual ones for show-and-tell. But there are all these dozens left!

Okay, let's assume that we have sold you on this shellcraft thing and that you are now willing and eager to get into it. You begin by sorting the shells. We don't want to discourage you, but we're pretty certain you'll find that only a few of those you have collected at random can be used for crafts. The medium and small whelks will make cute little pelicans, with kitten's paws for feet. The lucinas will make excellent flower petals. The olives and bubble shells look like good flower buds and centers, but the sizes of these are not uniform and we do not have enough of one size and color even for the petals of one flower! Collecting then should be our first order of business.

Collecting Shells for Shellcraft

Before your next trip to the beach, figure out what shells you need for the articles you wish to make, and then as you roam the sands, keep a look-out for them. Over the years, craftsmen have settled on certain shells as being the most applicable for certain purposes, so it would be wise to start with these, and then as you acquire skill, branch out and use your imagination.

For example, abalones were used as jewel boxes by craftsmen of the past. The ugly, mossy layer that usually covers them was scraped away, and they were carefully polished to bring out their lovely colors. Then the two sides were hinged, and presto—a beautiful jewel box.

Abalones are also a source of mother-of-pearl. There is only one species on the Atlantic coast, but the Pacific has several. You may have to purchase them from shell dealers, for these creatures, valuable both as food and for their shells, were almost wiped out by commercial collectors. There is now a limit set on the numbers and sizes you may collect. Check the local regulations before you begin to collect abalones.

The shell of the pearl oyster is also a source of mother-of-pearl. These oysters can be found in the Pacific and Indian Oceans, on the coast of Australia and in the Persian Gulf.

Helmet shells were and are used for cameos because they are made up of several layers of different colors. The best cameos are made in Africa and Italy. You can sometimes find them in some of the better jewelry shops.

Many shells have multiple uses in crafts. For instance, a small slipper shell (or boat shell) can miraculously turn into an animal. With the addition of tiny, ear-shaped, pinkish shells (coquinas or rose cups), black seed eyes and nose and a rubber band tail, you have a cute mouse. The slipper shell may also serve as a jaunty hat for a small critter, or even as a flower bud or petals on a flat floral arrangement. Several lucinas, of like size and color, may become the petals of a lotus blossom, magnolia or rose, or with curved side up, a water lily pad.

Both bivalves (shells with matching halves that are hinged together) and univalves (single shells) are used in shellcraft. Bivalves of all sizes are used for flower petals, from the big magnolia blossom to the tiny spray flowers. Univalves often make excellent buds and centers for these flowers.

So decide on what you want to make, study the shells needed and then search specifically for them. But of course, keep an open mind—there will be times when the sea withholds that certain something you want while lavishly bestowing other treasures which will serve as well.

When hunting for shells, keep your project in mind. For instance, if you find a smooth, white, petal-shaped shell, hunt for more of the same size and color; when you have from four to a dozen of them, you have a flower. The number of petals, of course, depends upon the type of flower you want to make. When you come upon a medium-sized whelk shell, picture it as a critter's body and hunt for a smaller one for the head. Then when you find the right size kitten's paws or slipper shells for feet, you have the makings for an animal or bird. A large olive shell looks like the body of a penguin. Start from there and find wings, feet and an auger or wentletrap shell for a head.

As you can see, it is important to study the pictures of the objects you wish to make. Then keep a lookout for the components as you beachcomb. This is not to say that only the shells used by others are suitable for the item you wish to create. Substitute shells may prove even more applicable and will individualize your work. The pictures in this and other books on shell-

Fig. 2.1 Shells (left to right, top to bottom): Row 1: Calico clam, docina, sand dollar, cupped scallop, cockle, lucina (face shell). Row 2: Whelk egg sack, horseshoe crab, crab, operculum, sea urchin, sea horse, starfish, cow fish. Row 3: Moon snail, bonnet shell, paper whelk, conch, whelk, fluted conch (or bud shell), cerithium, olive. Row 4: Mississippi bluefer, flat scallop, sunray venus, king crown, tulip shell.

Fig. 2.2 Shells (left to right, top to bottom): Row 1: White coral, gar scales, snails, squilla claws, rice shells (dyed), lilac shells (dyed). Row 2: Dogwood shell, buttercup, coquinas, cup shells (these four sizes are listed in catalog as "extra large, large, medium, and small"). Row 3: Turkey wing, Florida jewel box, worm casing, augers, cowries, bubble. Row 4: Purple clam, pearly clam, pink clam, limpet, slipper shell, jingle shell.

craft are merely patterns to help you in your choice and to get you started.

You must learn to identify the most widely used shells. Cockles, limpets, slipper shells, jingle shells, mussels, whelks, rose cups, olives, tellins, coquinas, clams, lucinas, snails, barnacles and cowries will do for a start (see Figs. 2.1 and 2.2).

There is one problem here—many of these shells will be occupied by live animals that must be removed. This is an unpleasant job which we try to avoid. Chapter 3 provides information on removal of live animals from shells in case you find it necessary to undertake this task.

Don't overlook anything in your search, but don't be too greedy either; others will be roaming those beaches. It is a good ecological practice to try to find unoccupied shells. Collecting occupied shells can, and in some cases did, wipe some species from our waters.

Poisonous Sea Animals

Caution is the word when collecting live shells, for some of them are poisonous. Some cone shells can give a painful, and with certain species a deadly, sting. When wading, watch out for those beautiful blue balloons

floating in the water—these tell you the Portuguese man-of-war is drifting there (see Fig. 2.3). When those tentacles (some of them as much as sixty feet long) wrap around your ankle, the sting can cause excruciating pain. We had this happen to us in Hawaii and know whereof we speak! The poison is potent enough to cause the death of a good-sized fish. The man-of-war's blue bubble acts as a sail, and he drifts helplessly with the wind. For this reason, you sometimes find these creatures cast up on the beach by the hundreds. It could be extremely dangerous to go into the water at that point.

Fig. 2.3 This Portuguese man-of-war has drifted up on the beach—an excellent warning not to go wading.

Fig. 2.4 Scooting the feet along, when wading and shelling, could prevent a painful sting from the barb of a stingray such as this.

Some swimming beaches fly a flag of warning when the man-of-war are in; they are considered almost as dangerous as sharks.

Another rascal to watch out for when wading is the stingray (see Fig. 2.4). It will lie almost buried in the sand with the hard point of the stinger on its tail erect and ready to pierce the unwary foot. A safe way to wade is to wear shoes of some sort (we like canvas) and to scoot your feet as you walk. This is also a good idea in water where sea urchins abound (see Fig. 2.5). You may not notice them, as they have a clever little habit of plastering themselves with the empty shells of other creatures for camouflage. Seeing that nice batch of shells, you may be tempted to pick it up. Don't! Friends who have stepped on one have had their day ruined by a trip to the doctor.

Collecting Other Items

Wherever shells are found, there will also be a wide variety of other items that can add interest and authenticity to your artwork, especially to the sea and beach scenes. So, as you watch for the shells you want, don't overlook the odd pieces of driftwood and coral, or the net corks and sea-aged   11 knots of rope (see Fig. 2.6). Also keep a lookout for the flora and weedlike fauna of the sea—these add tremendously to pictures and arrangements (see Fig. 2.7 and Color Plates). Even strange little things have their uses. For example, a cupped shell encrusted with barnacles will make a cute Easter bonnet for a little girl critter.

Every item you want will not necessarily be lying out where you can see it. Among the drifts of shells will be gloppy stuff that looks like nothing of interest. However, when pushed apart with a stick it may yield treasures missed by other shellers. The rascally little coquinas, which have so many uses, are odd creatures who live in colonies at the edge of the water and busily bury themselves in the sand with the passing of each wave. You will, of course, find large numbers of empty coquina shells looking like colorful little butterflies on the beach, but if you want to collect some of them alive, it is easy to scoop them up with handfuls of sand as the waves recede.

As you search the shallows, look among the grasses for snails and other small shellfish. Don't overlook the fact that objects could have been carried far up onto the sand dunes by storms. It is here that you may find the bony

Fig. 2.5 Some sea urchins have poisonous spines that can inflict a painful wound.

Fig. 2.6 A walk on the beach at dusk is always a soul-satisfying experience, and sometimes one has the additional bonus of finding drifts of treasures such as this.

Fig. 2.7 We used a wide variety of seedpods, sea whips, sea oats and shells to make
these attractive panels. They are flat arrangements and are glued to velure
paper.

Fig. 2.8 Cut shells can be purchased at most shell shops and can be used in endless creative designs such as the sprays on these two plaques.

skeletons of fish and spiny sea urchins. These make good centers for some types of flowers.

Note too the things that may be found even farther up on the beach. There will be sea oat sprays (though it is illegal in some areas to pick them), driftwood and land snails. Search under coconut trees for the lovely little wood roses that are actually the buds of immature coconuts which have broken off in high winds. Collect some of those little prickly cones from the Australian pines. These may all be combined with shells, purchased cut shells (see Fig. 2.8), sea flora and fauna and other seed sprays and pods, to make attractive pictures and arrangements.

3

Preparing Shells for Use

As we have said, it is best to collect empty shells. However, the shells needed for a certain item might not always be available in a vacated state. This leaves you with three choices—you can abandon the project, buy the shells you need or collect shells that contain live animals. For those who wish to purchase shells, suppliers' names and addresses are listed at the end of the book. The following paragraphs should help those who have had to collect shells containing live animals.

Removing Live Animals

There are several ways to kill live shellfish quickly, but one of the best and fastest is to place the shells in warm water and then boil them for about ten minutes. For very small shells, such as coquinas, the cooking time is less; very large shells may take more than ten minutes (see Fig. 3.1). Now lift the shells out of the water with tongs, being careful not to break them. The meat can now be pulled out easily with an ice pick or some other sharp tool (see Fig. 3.2).

Hermit crabs can easily be removed from the shells they are occupying. Plunge the shell into boiled fresh water that is just cool enough for you to put your hand in it. Boiling removes oxygen from the water so the crab will dash out of his shell to find air.

Fig. 3.1 This is the large, barnacle-covered horse conch that we had to clean. It looked hopeless at first sight, but with persistence we cleaned it up nicely. The first step was a thirty-minute boiling.

Fig. 3.2 After the boiling, we could remove the meat. This one came out easily but an ice pick or screw driver may sometimes be needed for a lever. By the way, conchs and whelks are edible, though rather rubbery.

Bleaching

Now examine the shells for defects. Badly eroded shells will have to be discarded, especially if they are to be used for flowers. Some shells will need more cleaning than others. Barnacles and other encrustations must be scraped off (see Fig. 3.3). Even some of the shells you purchased from dealers may not have bee well cleaned and may need attention. If the shells are in good condition after scraping, a soap and water bath followed by a rinse in clear water will be all that is needed.

Some weathered, rough, dead-white shells require more drastic measures (see Fig. 3.4). Soaking them in a twenty percent solution of bleach (Clorox® or Purex®) often brings out the natural colors, but heavily encrusted shells may require a stronger solution (fifty percent, or even full strength). Check the shells often as they soak. Strong bleach will remove the limy, crusty look, but it can fade colors if overdone.

Using Muriatic Acid

Try scraping or sanding shells that are coated with that tenaciously clinging skin called periostracum. If these methods fail, soak the shells in a solution of muriatic acid. But use caution: this acid can cause severe burns (it can eat holes in metal). You can easily ruin a valuable shell with muriatic acid, for it can dull the rich gloss of the shell's interior. For this reason, it is wise to coat the glossy parts of shells with hot paraffin before treating them with muriatic acid.

Fig. 3.3 Next, we scraped and scrubbed the shell to remove the barnacles.

Fig. 3.4 To remove the dark coating on the shell put it in a muriatic acid or bleach bath.

Fig. 3.5 If the edges of a shell are chipped, they can be ground down. Here a workman at The Shell Factory, near Ft. Myers, Florida, demonstrates this process.

Choose a container that will not be affected by the acid (glass is good) and mix a solution of about ½ cup of muriatic acid per gallon of water. Using tongs, dip the shells into the solution one at a time. For badly encrusted shells, you may need a stronger solution. Leave the shell in the solution only a few seconds—the acid will quickly eat holes in fragile shells. Now plunge the shell into a cold water rinse to stop the action of the acid. If further treatment seems to be called for, wash the shells in soapy water and then brush them with a sponge or brush. Now rinse them again.

Finishing

The edges of shells are sometimes chipped. These edges can be smoothed by grinding, as illustrated in Figure 3.5.

You can brighten the colors of shells to be used in a display collection by rubbing them with baby oil. But this is not necessary if the shell is to be dyed or lacquered. If the baby oil you use seems too thick and heavy, mix it with a little lighter fluid. The lighter fluid will evaporate leaving only a thin coating of oil. Polish the shell well so that the oil will not collect dust. You can now use the shell however you wish (see Figs. 3.6 and 3.7).

Fig. 3.6 The cleaned conch was a lovely rose shade.

Fig. 3.7 Our friend, Margaret Elgersman, made a macrame hanger for a conch and then used it for a hanging planter.

Sorting

Now that the shells are clean, let's get organized for the artwork. It is much more enjoyable to work when the shells have been sorted by color, size and type (see Fig. 3.8). If you have a nice big table for a work area, lay the shells out in rows at the back, leaving the front space for your work area.

For some items, you might want to keep your hinged shells paired, but for flower petals it is better to have the right and left sides in separate piles. Sort the tiny shells such as baby whelks, little lilacs and coquinas, and put them in small jars or plastic boxes to prevent breakage. You will also want your various kinds of seeds in separate see-through containers. The cupped

Fig. 3.8 After collecting, sort your shells by type, color and size.

compartments of plastic-coated egg cartons are also excellent containers for small items. Sort the seaweeds and other sea growths and put them in cardboard boxes to prevent damage.

If the seaweeds that you plan to use are tangled and matted and too stiff to straighten out satisfactorily, soak them in water and, when they have softened, lay them out on paper in whatever arrangement you desire and allow them to dry. An authentic touch may be added to underwater scenes by arranging the branches swept over in one direction so that they look exactly as they do when they're in the water.

Much of the flora and fauna you collect will be studded with hitchhikers, such as barnacles and other sea creatures. Leave them on if the shells or plants are to be used in scenes—they add realism.

21

Dyeing Shells

Dyeing shells may prove to be rather frustrating. There is such a predominance of white shells, and so few colorful ones, that we decided to dedicate some time to finding dyes or paints that would produce at least a reasonable facsimile of the real thing. We must sadly report that, at this writing, we are still seeking dyes or paints that produce the delicate, translucent shades that occur in nature.

We experimented at first with cloth dyes. But even though we used several different methods (boiling, hot bath, adding vinegar), none was satisfactory. For one thing, the shells tended to get blotchy. The dyes penetrated the limy areas, but failed to penetrate those that were glossy. Of course in some cases, this variegated effect gave a rather natural look.

We then tried food coloring thinking that the dyes that colored Easter eggs so beautifully might also color shells. No go! In most cases, the shells came out as white as they went in. Then we added vinegar, as recommended for eggs. This worked slightly better, but it dulled the shells. Of course you could restore the gloss with a clear spray varnish or lacquer, but the poor coloring hardly merits all that trouble.

Next we experimented with our artist's oils, but this was an even greater fiasco. The opaque colors simply made gaudy, painted shells. The translucent oils (lake colors) were somewhat better. We found that it was possible to get some rather interesting effects with these oils by shading a shell from very light at the edges to dark at the hinges. For this process, put puddles of oils on your palette and mix in a lot of turpentine or paint thinner. The turpentine helps the paint to penetrate the shells. Paint the shells with this thin mixture and then let them sit a few minutes. Then wipe off most of the paint with a paper towel. Though this was the best method we found, the coloring still was not as even as we had hoped it would be.

Shading shells with a flat, spray paint can (with practice) give them a natural look (see Fig. 3.9), but a solid coat of opaque paint, though it may make them the color of the flowers we are attempting to duplicate, gives shells the appearance of plastic flowers. It was for this reason that we conducted such time-consuming experiments on dyeing shells. We thought that dyes would not obscure the shells, as paint most certainly does.

Pearl essence, or colored lacquer, more closely approximates the colors of shells. This is not opaque and gives colorless or dull shells a nice, iridescent color without obscuring their natural coloring. This lacquer comes in flower shades and may be either sprayed or brushed on. We like to use a brush as it allows us to shade the colors in a manner natural to both shells and flowers.

Fig. 3.9 Our shell dyeing was a dismal failure, but a lady at The Shell Factory showed us that spraying with a flat paint can be very effective. She displayed a remarkable skill at shading flowers in this way.

For example, a peace rose is a lovely yellow shade with an edging of pink, and some shells closely approximate its coloration. Fluted conches may be a soft yellow white on the outside and a pearly pink at the edge of the furl and on the inside. Though these make amazingly natural-looking rosebuds, it is difficult to find enough of them. So we tried the pearl lacquer, first brushing the inside and lip of the furl a rosy pink and then brushing the outside yellow. Though this bud may be slightly brighter in color than those found in the natural state, it does not offend the sensibilities; it is, at least, a close resemblance. We have also lacquered white rosebuds with rose-colored centers and used white pearl lacquer to brighten and enliven aged, limy-looking shells.

23

Pearl essence can be used on all types of flowers that have naturally glossy petals. For flowers with thin delicate petals, such as the daisy, zinnia and poppy, the non-gloss, clear lacquer spray works best. It protects and enlivens, but it doesn't give these naturally non-glossy flowers a shiny look.

Some of the buds shown in our pictures were in such an excellent condition that we used them without any kind of treatment. Others (and we believe you can easily tell which) have been sprayed with pearl essence or clear lacquer. It is a matter of individual choice. We offer these examples and suggestions so that by studying them you can more easily decide for yourself.

Strangely enough, none of the shell catalogs we happen to have, list shell dyes, yet each offers a rather wide variety of dyed shells. Why don't they sell the dyes? Is it possible that these companies have shell dyeing secrets that they don't reveal? Perhaps the companies are safeguarding their incomes, for if their customers could dye shells they would make use of the ones they had collected.

A great many of the shellcraft items we see for sale have been sprayed with a flat paint so that they appear to be shaded. The blue dress of the doll in Figure 8.13 and the pink pond lily centerpiece in Figure 5.11 were both done in this manner. Though they don't have the look of shell, they are rather pretty.

Dyeing Fish Scales

Though not at all satisfied with our shell dyeing experiments, we had glorious success with dyeing fish scales that were to be used in making flowers and leaves.

For leaves, we settled on forest green Rit® with hopes that this shade would give a natural leaf color. It proved to be exactly the color we were seeking. The dyeing operation was, however, a time-consuming job. After dyeing, we rinsed and separated the many little scales and spread them out on paper towels to dry. We covered them with more towels and weighted the whole thing down with a board to prevent the scales from curling as they dried. A slight curl is sometimes desirable as real flower petals and leaves often cup or curve. But, if scales are left to dry on their own, they are likely to curl too much. We did find, however, that even after they have dried, soaking overly cupped scales in warm water for a few minutes and then weighting them down between paper towels will correct them.

Prepare the dye as directed on the box for cloth, and then allow it to cool slightly. Scales put in boiling water deteriorate badly, but warm water doesn't damage them. You may want to make the dye richer than for cloth.

The colors we liked best were made with about ½ package of dye to about 2 cups of water. Put the scales in the warm dyebath. Stir them often and test occasionally for tone. About twenty minutes usually suffices. Then dry them as described above. You can bottle your various dye colors and they will keep for about a week.

If you like to carry out the all-sea creature idea in your art, the fine bones of fish make excellent flower stems. These may be dyed along with the scales. The fishbones do not work well in free-standing bouquets; unlike wire, they can't be bent to the desired angles. But they work quite well glued directly to a background in flat pictures.

Some of our prettiest and most realistic flowers were made of large carp scales. Dyed maize and rose, they look exactly like fluffy poppies. Carp scales have one dark side. We turned this to the center to duplicate the dark center of a real poppy. Some peppercorns added to the realism.

Dyeing fish scales and bones is not really a laborious task. It might seem so at first thought, but you can dye a large amount at one time. Make it a point to dye various sizes of scales and bones at the same time, and then store them for future use. In this way there will be no delay once you actually start to make your flowers.

As a summary on dyeing: dye scales and bones, and if you find a good method for dyeing shells, let us know about it—please!

Fig. 4.1 Most of the supplies and tools needed for shell art are pictured here. In addition to these, we use a small, electric drill for grinding edges and drilling holes.

4

Tools and Supplies

The next order of business is assembling the tools and supplies. It may seem from this lengthy listing that an overpowering number of materials are needed, but when you examine the list you will find that many of the items, such as pliers, tweezers and cotton, are already among your household or shop supplies (see Fig. 4.1).

List of Tools

Side cutters. For cutting wire.
Small electric drill.
Long-nosed pliers. For twisting wire.
Tongs. For lifting shells from bleach.
Tweezers. For handling small objects.
Vise. This item is not absolutely necessary.

List of Supplies

Baby oil. This will brighten shells.
Bleach. Any good bleach will deodorize and clean shells.
Chenille wire or pipe cleaners. These are used in several ways, primarily in the making of shell animals and birds (see Chapter 7) and rings on which to glue flowers.

Cotton. Cotton is a much-needed commodity in shellcraft. Mixed thoroughly with glue, cotton provides a strong bonding agent and forms a porcelain-like substance when dry. Use as little cotton as possible; it should not show.

Disks. Plastic and mother-of-pearl disks can be purchased at hobby shops in sizes ranging from ⅜ to 1 inch.

Dye. Cloth dyes, Rit® or Tintex®, though not very satisfactory for shells, work well on fish scales. Instructions for the preparation and use of dye are included in Chapter 3.

Ear clips or screws. Undecorated bases for earrings are available at hobby shops. Flowers or other decorations may either be glued directly to them or affixed with a bit of glue-soaked cotton. You may also construct your decoration on a small plastic disk and glue it to the ear clip when dry. We prefer the latter method.

Elastic and chains. We use round elastic and chains to make necklaces and bracelets. Drill holes in the shells and thread the elastic through them with a large darning needle. Necklaces and bracelets are great for children to make.

Eyes. Plastic, rolling eyes add a comical and appealing aspect to shell critters. They can be purchased at hobby shops in several sizes. You can paint eyes on your critters, too.

Florist clay. We use green florist clay in several ways. One use is for welding blocks of Styrofoam® firmly in the bottoms of vases and other containers so we can push flower stems into the Styrofoam at any angle with the assurance that it will not tilt. Also, using small bits of this clay to temporarily hold flowers and other items to backgrounds allows you to study their arrangement before fastening them permanently.

Florist tape. Most tape is less than ½ inch wide, stretchy and slightly sticky. We use both green and brown tape—the green for wrapping the stems of flowers and the brown for woody-type stems.

Glue. Orinoco® cement works well for us. It is fast-drying and dries clear. However, realizing that this glue cannot be purchased everywhere, we tried out several other kinds. Tacky® and several other brands work almost as well as Orinoco. The important thing is to use a glue that dries quickly and is thick and clear.

Jars and plastic boxes. Clear, see-through containers, as well as plastic egg cartons, are fine for holding and storing the small shells, seeds and other tiny items needed in shellcraft.

Lacquer spray or varnish. A coat of clear lacquer or clear varnish protects finished shell items, waterproofs them so they may be cleaned and lessens the fading of colors.

Leaves and ferns. It would be great if floral arrangements could be made up of only those things that come from the sea, but unfortunately, the green leaves which add so much to the appearance of these arrangements are hard to come by in shells! We use fish scales whenever we can get them (they can be bought at shell shops) and artificial foliage only when we cannot. If you must use artificial foliage (plastic or velvet), you can use either only the plastic stems (with shell flowers replacing the artificial flowers) or only the leaves (which can then be wired or wrapped on your wire stems).

Muriatic acid. This is a tricky liquid to use; it can cause painful burns. For this reason we seldom use it, but a treatment in muriatic acid can improve some discolored and heavily coated shells. Bleach will be sufficient for most of your needs.

Pins. Brooch pins come in many sizes and can be purchased at all hobby shops. The same methods are followed in decorating brooches as are used for decorating earrings (see Chapter 11).

Thread. Strong nylon thread is excellent for stringing shells or shell beads for necklaces.

Toothpicks. You will find many uses for these humble items, from pushing tiny seeds and shells into place to wiping away excess glue.

Wire. Three sizes of wire will provide for all your needs. We like green-coated wire in gauge sizes from 18 to 28. We use the finer wire (28 gauge) for clusters and sprays of small flowers and for fish scale leaves; a slightly larger green wire for wiring heavier, individual blossoms; and the 18 gauge wire for main stems.

Work board. A roll-up plastic breadboard or other heavy plastic sheet makes a great work board, but plastic bowl lids and plastic plates work as well. You form flowers and other items on the plastic work sheet and then when dry they are easily removed by slipping a knife under them.

5

Shell Flower Making

To make accurate flowers, you may study garden magazines and attempt to duplicate the gorgeous flowers pictured there or follow the techniques used by the master shell-art craftsmen of past eras. The following pages first give general flower making directions and then detailed instructions for constructing individual flowers.

For flowers less than an inch across, squeeze a puddle of glue out on your work sheet for a base. Larger flowers, using heavier shells, require more substantial bases. Plastic disks or pipe cleaner rings of varying sizes should be used, especially for free-standing flowers. When choosing what size disk to use, consider the size of the petals and use a base that will not show when the flower is finished. If flowers are to be glued directly to a background, it is still wise to make them on the plastic work sheet; when dry, you can move them around on the sheet to study their arrangement before the final gluing.

A small pipe cleaner ring filled with glue-soaked cotton makes a good base. Either use a green pipe cleaner or one the color of the flower or touch it up with paint when dry. To attach petals to the base, put glue on the end of each one and then push them into the glue-soaked cotton. Start with the outermost ring of petals and then work toward the center, row by row. Use glue-soaked cotton to build up the base or center for double or fluffy flowers. When the glue-soaked cotton dries, it is almost as hard as porcelain.

Start at the outside ring of petals for flowers that are to be built up in the center. Then add more glue-soaked cotton to the middle, then another ring of petals, then more gluey cotton, and so on using increasingly smaller petals to the center.

The above method will not work well with very thick, heavy shell petals. You may have to wire heavy shells to perforated plastic disks to hold them upright.

For clusters or spikes of flowers, such as grape hyacinth or delphinium, use tiny or crushed shells. Here again wire and cotton come into the act. Loop a stem wire to accommodate the planned length of your cluster and, remembering always that the cluster or spiked flower head tapers at the top, shape glue-soaked cotton around the loop. Add more glue to the outside, and embed crushed or small shells in it before it dries. Coating the cotton thoroughly with glue not only holds the petals better but also makes the flower waterproof so that it may be washed when dirty. When the flower spike is dry, like all other flowers, it should be brushed or sprayed with lacquer.

You can follow these general instructions to make roses, apple blossoms, dogwood, daisies, buttercups, and many other blossoms. Single-petaled flowers, such as the wild rose and daisy, are made flatter and more open; double-petaled flowers, such as the tea rose, are usually more cupped and have many rows of petals. With some double-petaled flowers, the rows of petals are overlapping.

Creating sprays of flowers is intricate work that requires both patience and time. Graceful sprays add tremendously to the beauty and form of a mixed arrangement, and at least a few should be included.

Centers and leaves will be dealt with in detail later in this chapter, but generally these are a matter of personal choice. If you are a purist who wants only items from the sea in your arrangements, you may dye and use several kinds of shells or operculums (trapdoors) of univalves or make sprays of large, dyed fish scales. Other types of possible foliage which come from the sea are the sea flora and fauna, such as sea fans, sea whips and sea ferns. These make interesting additions to flower arrangements.

Tiny univalves, such as baby whelks and snails, or various kinds of seed may be used for centers. Yellow mustard seeds, black seeds such as peppercorns and cloves—all may be used.

This then is the general composition and instruction for flower making. The following pages give detailed instructions for making some of the best-known flowers.

Stems

There are three types of shell flower arrangements: free-standing, espaliered and flat. Free-standing arrangements are like conventional fresh flower bouquets. They will usually be placed in a bowl, vase or very deep shadow box. Espaliered, narrow-depth arrangements are done against a background in medium-shallow shadow boxes, in convex-glassed frames, and on plaques. In flat arrangements, the flowers, stems and foliage are glued directly to the background material. These can be made in very shallow shadow boxes, convex-glassed frames or unglassed pictures. All can be lovely, and your only limitation is that of fitting the type of arrangement you choose to the materials you have to work with.

Free-standing arrangements are the most difficult and time-consuming to make as most of the flowers must be wired or fastened to some sort of stem. Some of the smaller, individual flowers do not have to be constructed directly on a stem. You can make them on your plastic work board, let them dry and then glue them to the stems. The larger flowers that are made of heavier shells will have to have holes drilled into them for wiring, and they must be constructed on a stem.

If a flower is small to medium and has a single univalve center (see Fig. 5.8), wiring the center, without wiring the petals, may suffice. With the addition of some thin bits of glue-soaked cotton as fill-in material, the petals for this size flower may be glued directly to the center. If the shells are very heavy and large, it is best to wire each petal, arrange them around the center, bring all the wires together and twist. Then glue-soaked cotton may be pushed into the openings where the petals come together at the base.

Green plastic calyxes are great for covering up wiring. Hobby shops that sell flower-making materials have several sizes of these. The calyx has a hole through it so you can easily slip it on the end of the wire and then pull it up to fit snugly around the lower part of the flower. A little glue will hold it securely. A calyx at the base of a single bud also gives it a finishing touch that lends realism. The wire stem will be wrapped with green florist tape. Put glue on the wire first, then wrap.

For flowers that are light to medium in weight, there are a number of other ways to make stems. All these may be made on your plastic work sheet and glued onto the wire after they are dry. The basic methods are shown here (see Figs. 5.1–5.3).

1. The coiled wire, platform stem, first on the left in Figure 5.1, is merely a straight section of wire with a flat coil on top to which a single flower is glued (with the addition of a cotton-soaked pad).

2. For added stability, the second stem from the left has a circle of pipe cleaner twisted in with it. Here again, gluey cotton gets into the act. The circle is filled with it, and the flower is glued on.

3. The third stem pictured has a plastic disk wired to it. Glue the flower to the disk with the usual pad of glue-soaked cotton.

Fig. 5.1 These are four of the eleven ways we form flower stems. The first stem on the left is used most. The fourth stem from the left is a long loop covered with glue-soaked cotton that is used to make spike flowers.

Fig. 5.2 Four more stem forms on which both flowers and leaves can be glued.

33

Fig. 5.3 Three more flower stems. The first on the left is used for a heavy flower petal, the second for clusters, and the third is a plastic stem with leaves, from which the plastic flower has been removed so that a shell flower can be glued in its place.

4. The last stem in Figure 5.1 is for spikes of flowers. This is just a straight piece of wire with a long loop bent in the end on which glue-soaked cotton has been pressed. Form the cotton into a point at the top and glue the tiny petals or crushed shell to it before it dries.

5. The first stem on the left in Figure 5.2 is for a bushy type of flower with multiple blossoms. Bunch a number of fine wires together, tie them near one end and then bend out each wire at a different height. Clip the wires to the lengths desired remembering always to allow extra wire for the coils at the ends. Proceed to glue on flowers as described for the single coil stem. Wrap with florist tape.

6. Double-wire branches can be made by bending out one long wire in twisted loops to form branches (second stem from the left, Fig. 5.2).

After doubling and twisting a branch, bring the wire back to form the center stem, and so on up to where the top branch extends at the highest point. You will have to cover all the stems with a thin coating of glue and wrap them with florist tape.

7. Artificial foliage is of course the easiest way to supply stems for your flowers. The artificial stem shown in Figure 5.2 is the "pop-off" type. The plastic flowers may be pulled from the knob and replaced by shell flowers. If the flowers are small, a wad of glue-soaked cotton may be wrapped around the end of the knob, spread out and flattened to become a base for the flowers. When dry, it may be touched up with green paint, with paint the color of the petals or a calyx may be pulled up to cover the base.

8. For buds and centers made of univalves, drill a hole in the lower, closed end (see fourth stem from the left in Fig. 5.2), push a wad of gluey cotton along with the end of the wire into the hole and allow it to dry. As in some other flowers, an artificial calyx improves the appearance.

9. The first stem on the left in Figure 5.3 shows what to do if flower petals are heavy. Drill two holes in the base of each petal, loop wire through them and then twist the wire. After the flower is complete, the long sepals of a calyx will hide the wires nicely.

10. For flowers that have clusters of small blossoms in each flower head, use a perforated plastic disk (one to two inches across, depending on the type of flower). Wire the disk with stem wire as in the second stem in Figure 5.3. Now make the individual flowers using fine wire. Push the stems of the individual flowers through the holes in the disk and bring all the ends of the wires in to the center stem. Wrap the stem with florist tape.

Cluster flowers, of a looser type, can be made with a bundle-stem method (see Figs. 5.16 and 5.17). A bundle of thin wires is bound together and wrapped with florist tape, then splayed out at the ends to form a rounded cluster shape, with each end of the fine wires coiled to accommodate a blossom.

11. The third stem from the left in Figure 5.3 shows a calyx in place on a stem. You would not actually add the calyx until you had completed the flower.

Rose

Olive or bubble shells make good buds and centers for most roses. You may have to grind the point flat or drill it before you can wire or glue these shells. If the rose is to be wired (and very heavy ones should be), push a small piece of glue-soaked cotton into the hole with the stem wire. It will dry and harden to hold the stem firmly.

All the components for roses to be made directly on a background, on a plastic disk or on a pipe cleaner ring, should be assembled and ready before any glue is applied to the base (the glue dries very quickly). This precaution should be taken with all flowers.

Once the center of a double rose is glued, lap petals around it putting glue on each petal and then pushing them down into the glue-soaked cotton. Continue until the rose is the desired size. The middle petals should be upright around the center, with the others gradually tilting out until the outer petals are almost horizontal. Don't forget that the older outer petals of full-blown roses curl in reverse. For these, glue the outer edge of petals with their cupped side down. To make semi-double roses, simply use fewer petals than you use for the double roses.

Large white or pink rose cup shells or jingle shells are fine for roses. The colors of jingle shells vary greatly, and if enough of one color cannot be found, you can shade the rose. Try one with deep salmon pink at the center shading to pale yellow at the outer edges. Cockles make attractive large roses, but you may have to dye them to get the best effect.

Single roses are made as above but with only one row of petals, and with the hinges, or rolled edge, at the outer tips to give the effect of curled petals. Single roses and wild roses usually do not have a tight bud center. For these, use three or more open petals at the center with a cluster of tiny whelks, yellow lilac shells, yellow mustard seeds, or black seeds glued in the middle.

Some craftsmen prefer to start the flower at the outer edge and work in. We like this method for some types of flowers, but for roses, starting in the center works best for us (see Fig. 5.4).

If the shells used for petals are heavy, drill two holes in the base of each one, then wire it and glue it to a perforated plastic disk. Bring all the wires together at the base of the flower and wrap them with a wad of glue-soaked cotton. If it is to be a free-standing flower, twist the finer wires around the heavy stem wire (that was previously glued into the center). Now wrap the rose stem with green florist tape from the lower end right on up over the cotton at the lower part of the rose. At this point the leaves would be wrapped in with the stem, but we will describe this method later (see the paragraph on *Clusters and Spikes* in this chapter).

Daisy

As a general rule, daisies, brown-eyed susans and other flowers of this type have a single row of petals, though the actual number of petals varies, and a large flat or rounded center. Rice shells or small olives, with their open-

Fig. 5.4 The steps for making a shell rose: from a pad of glue-soaked cotton to the completed flower. Roses are made on a plastic work sheet. When the glue is dry, the blossom may be glued to a coiled stem wire with a bit of gluey cotton.

ing showing, make excellent petals for the type that have curled petals, and coquinas, with their many colors, are fine for the flatter petal type. Make the centers of yellow-dyed crushed shells or gar scales. For some types, a small black trapdoor, or even a mat of black or dark brown seeds, slightly domed with gluey cotton, makes a good center. The trapdoors, or operculums, are found on live univalves or washed up on shore, but you may also purchase them in various sizes from shell suppliers. The only problem in using these shells is that they are seldom perfectly round, and are most often a pointed oval.

One of the most attractive shell daisies is a brown-eyed susan made of natural-colored or dyed yellow coquinas with a dark (brown or black) seed cluster or dark operculum center. Glue coquinas around a pipe cleaner-cotton base (or plastic disk), then glue the center on the slightly rounded, glue-soaked cotton in the middle. We like to use a center made of a cluster of yellow mustard seeds for white daisies.

Carnation

The fluted shells called kitten's paws make very realistic carnations, dahlias, pinks and other fluffy flowers, but some other shells resemble these and serve almost as well. As in the daisies, build these flowers on a pipe cleaner-cotton ring or plastic disk. Begin with the larger petals on the outside ring and use ever smaller shells as you near the center, as the center petals actually develop last. Slant the outside petals almost flat, raising the progressing circle until the middle cluster is erect. If you don't have enough of the exact size shells, those that are too short can be built up with a bit of gluey cotton.

Carnations have a trumpet-shaped calyx which may be formed with glue-soaked cotton after the flower is dry and then painted green. You may also use a plastic calyx, which can be purchased in any hobby shop that sells flower parts.

Coquinas, or other small, narrow shells (use the hump or hinge at the base) make excellent dahlias and zinnias. Baby whelks or lilacs can be used for the very smallest flowers.

Dogwood

Dogwood shell flowers made of four white lucinas or rose cups look quite real. The hinged sides of these shells look exactly like the oddly cupped lips of dogwood petals (see Fig. 5.5). To add to the illusion, touch up these tips with a bit of thin brown paint or dye. Remember that this is a woody plant and the branches are to be wrapped with brown florist tape. The dogwood differs from many flowers in that the blossoms come on before the leaves, so you may make them leafless. However, the light green leaves appear before the blossoms fall, so using leaves is acceptable as well.

On the tree, dogwood sprays face up toward the sun in tiered levels, but when one of these branches is arranged in a vase, all the flowers face front.

Forming the flowers on a wired or unwired disk, or pipe cleaner ring, lap the petals slightly, but lay them out almost flat. Make the centers out of clusters of any tiny, yellow-dyed shells with the points down, and the bud-like open ends up. If you have made the flowers on your plastic work sheet, they should now be glued to a fine coiled wire. Now use brown florist tape to wrap these wires in as sprays on a heavier stem wire.

We experimented with the use of real dogwood branches for these and were well pleased with the effect. However, the hard, tough wood of a manzanita tree is best. It seems to last forever and has a lovely, satiny deep red

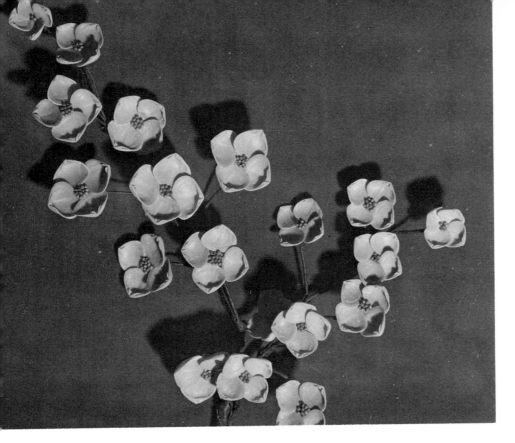

Fig. 5.5 A spray of pink dogwood. The stems are wrapped with brown florist tape so they will be realistic.

shade that adds tremendously to the beauty of an arrangement. Manzanita branches can be purchased at florist's shops in sizes ranging from a small twig to large branches several feet long.

Lotus

The lotus, or pond lily, and the magnolia are probably the largest flowers you will want to make. They are also among the loveliest, forming beautiful centerpieces and wall plaques. Some of these plaques, made up of a dozen or more flowers, are from two to five feet in length.

The magnolia is usually used on a tray or flat dish. It is difficult to duplicate their pointed leaves with shells, but you may surround them with large plastic leaves. Operculums (the long, pointed kind) can be dyed a dark green and used, but they are rather expensive if you must buy them. If you use operculums for the leaves, wire them as shown in the stem-making section 39 and tape each one to a larger stem wire. Work down the stem wire until you have formed a thick, clustered spray. Group these in an oval and then nest the flower in the center. Make the flowers of dyed or white tellins or macoma shells.

Make two or three buds from whelk shells or fluted conchs (as shown in the Buds section), and wire in at the same time you wire in the flower.

You can also make a lotus using white, dyed yellow or dyed rose macoma clams or large tellins. Since these shells are large and rather heavy, they must be wired individually and then twisted together.

Flat green-dyed scallop shells make fine leaves and pads for the lotus, or pond lily. These too must be wired. If your scallops have hinges that are too prominent, grind them off or hide them under the edge of the flower.

Finish off both the magnolia and pond lily with the type of center needed for that kind of flower. Check pictures, for these vary. Seed catalogs or flower books are good, accurate sources. We like to use several different centers. We make one of them from a little cone of the Australian pine tree by simply clipping off the spines on one side and gluing this flat side to the center of the flower. Another nice center, especially for pond lilies, may be made by wrapping pads of glue-soaked cotton on wire, pressing a large amount of yellow-dyed crushed shells or yellow seeds into the glue and then using three of these spikes for a center.

Since both the magnolia and lotus have elongated petals, the hinge is turned to the side. Petals are lapped as you place them, with the center three or four forming an open bud around whatever center you are using.

Since the pond lily is probably one of the most difficult flowers you will make, it would probably be well to give a step by step description of the way we made the large one pictured in Figure 5.11. This centerpiece was quite difficult to make, but it turned out to be an impressive and lovely thing and so was worth the effort.

This lily was made of eleven pink Mississippi bluefers and the real difficulty lay in the fact that these were all the same size. We much prefer graduated sizes, using the small ones in the center, as in the deeper pink lily pictured in the color section. Also the bluefers are deeply cupped with a heavy lip, and this makes them more difficult to lap properly. Macomas, lucinas or shallower shells work better. However, we have learned to use what we have, and find a certain amount of satisfaction in working out the difficulties. Anyway, the results are what count, and the bluefer lily is attractive.

These shells are a natural pearly pink. For the center and buds we brushed on a pink pearl essence as near the natural color of the petals as we

Fig. 5.6 To make a large pond lily centerpiece, it is necessary to wire the heavy shells. First drill two holes in each shell petal.

could get. The lily pads are green-painted flat scallop shells with the hinges ground off. For this we used our little drill fitted with a grinding wheel.

For the petals, drill two holes in the lower end of the bluefer shells (see Fig. 5.6) and insert wires (gauge 21 is a good size). Then bring all four wires together and twist (see Fig. 5.7). After wiring all the petals, form five of them around the center bud (if this is the type of center you are using) and twist them together. Now lap the other six petals around these (see Fig. 5.8).

Make two or more buds as described in the bud section and wire them. Then twist their wires in with the petals. Now grind the hinges off of your three green shell leaves and drill two holes in each one. Proceed with the wiring as you did with the petals (see Figs. 5.9 and 5.10). Arrange the three pads in a three-leafed clover shape and place the flower on it. Twist all the wires together.

To finish off the stems, wrap the entire bundle with green florist tape. For neatness, glue a calyx to the base of the flower. We did not have a calyx large enough to cover such a large flower, so we cut two large plastic rose calyxes apart and fitted them around the base. A cloth calyx may be used just as successfully. We placed the completed centerpiece on a gracefully curved coconut bud shell, and the two complemented each other very nicely (see Fig. 5.11).

41

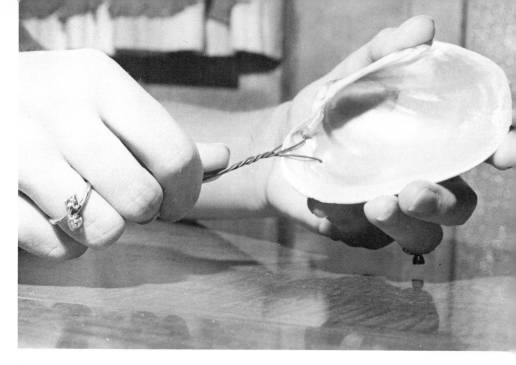

Fig. 5.7 Then insert one wire in each hole, double the wires and twist them together.

Fig. 5.8 With a previously wired fluted conch for a center, lap the smaller and then the larger petals around and pull all the wires together.

42

Fig. 5.9 To make the leaves (or pads), we ground off the hinges of three flat scallop shells and then sprayed them with green paint.

Fig. 5.10 The next step in making the pond lily leaves is to drill two holes at the base of each shell and wire them as we did with the petals. Arrange the leaves to lie flat around the flower and twist the wires with those of the petals.

43

Fig. 5.11 Then two wired buds are added, the wires are wrapped with florist tape, and the pond lily centerpiece is finished.

Fig. 5.12 The poppies and leaves pictured here are made entirely of dyed carp fish scales. The largest of these scales came from a fourteen-pound carp. Tarpon scales make beautiful, big flowers but are difficult to get.

44

Poppy

Jingle shells make excellent poppies. They are often found in a wide range of sunny colors, from deep orange to light yellow. Use a single, lapped row for single poppies. For the double type use your largest shells at the outer edge with smaller ones in another row inside. Form the flower on a pipe cleaner-cotton base or on a flattened pad of gluey cotton.

A small, cup-shaped shell or the coil end of an olive, cut off and dyed brown or black, makes a good center. You can also use the skeleton of a sea urchin shell's interior. These are often found washed up on the beach. When broken open, they reveal their stamenlike middle. Another good center for poppies is a forest of whole cloves or a cluster of peppercorns.

Yellow scallop shells and dyed cockles also make very attractive poppies. In some of the floral arrangements pictured in this book, we used carp scales, in natural white and dyed yellow and rose, for poppies. These are our favorites because they are so very natural looking (see Fig. 5.12).

Tulip

Tulips vary greatly in size and shape according to type. Here imagination plays a part. The shells you happen to have determine the kind of tulip you will make. Egg cockles and rose petals are good; mussels and lucinas make large tulips. Single barnacles or other tiny shells will serve for miniatures.

Lap three petals upright using a pipe cleaner-cotton ring or a flat disk of gluey cotton. Then glue three more around those with the edges at the center of the first ones. The center is not very apparent in deeply cupped tulips, but if it shows, a center of a darkish top shell or the cut point of a greyish olive can be used.

It would be difficult to duplicate the tulip's long, pointed leaves. If your tulips are to be used in an arrangement of other flowers, simply allow the leaves of the other flowers to serve as foliage. If you have some long, pointed operculums you might try dyeing them green and using them for leaves.

Fruit Blossoms

For fruit blossoms, envision the individual flowers as being about one inch across and proportion your lucina, rose cup, or jingle shell to that size. But of course if you are making all your flowers on a smaller scale than normal, these too would be smaller to correspond. Pear blossoms are a snowy

45

Fig. 5.13 Apple or pear blossoms made of shells are very realistic. Wrap their stems with brown florist tape to heighten the realism.

white, most apple blossoms are white or white touched with pink and peach blossoms are mostly pink.

Make each flower on your plastic work sheet, with a small plastic disk base and a bit of glue-soaked cotton, or in the case of very small blossoms, with only a puddle of glue. Actually, it is seldom necessary to use a disk or pipe cleaner ring as a base. A wad of cotton, thoroughly mixed with glue and spread out on the work sheet in a disk form, suffices for flowers that are as much as two inches across.

After the individual blossoms are dry, glue each of them to the coiled end of a stem made of 21 gauge green-coated wire. These can then be arranged in loose clusters and wired to a larger (18 gauge) wire.

Fruit blossoms, like the dogwood, are woody plants, and their stems should be wrapped with brown florist tape. Remember that sprays of any kind of flowers have smaller, more tightly closed blossoms at the ends of the twigs, so always make a few of these (see Fig. 5.13). Artificial plastic leaves or small branches of carp scale leaves may be wired in as you wrap the florist tape. For miniatures of woody plants, you might want to try using sea whips for branches or trunks (see Fig. 5.14 and color plates).

Buttercup

Here again yellow or orange jingle shells, or buttercup shells (so designated in shell shop catalogs), are used. Choose those shells that are the most cup shaped so that your flower will have the buttercup's natural appearance.

The center of the buttercup is an almost flat area. With this in mind, build the center up to a mesa in the following manner. Starting with a wired plastic disk, form a ball of glue-soaked cotton around the wire under the disk. Now start gluing the five petals. Press the hinge side up underneath so the shells cover the cotton. The center (plastic disk) is now from ¼ to ½ inch higher than the base of the petals, depending on the size of the flower. Now

Fig. 5.14 A flowering "tree" in a glass dome shelters a family of deer.

47

glue a cluster of stamens of any dark tiny shells into the center. Tiny whelks, with their points up, are good. Buttercup lucinas as well as jingles or small cockles may be used for the petals. Many of these are found in bright yellow and orange shades, though they are often blotched with black.

Pansy

Because the pansy's form is more stylized, its components require special selection. Shells for the two top petals must have a definite shape. Similar smaller shells are needed for the two petals on the sides and a round or wide oval is needed for the bottom petal. Almost any color can be used, for as you know, pansies bloom in a vast array of lovely shades. Nevertheless, the colors must be matched up in each pansy. For instance, if a right side top petal is a pale yellow, the corresponding left side petal must be the same shade. But then the three lower petals can all be a deep yellow or orange (as they are quite often in the natural flower). It is a good idea to study pansy pictures and try to duplicate them.

As a general rule, pansies have flat dark centers. The middle may be merely painted in with the touch of a brush dipped in dark dye or thinned paint, or it may consist of a cluster of black seeds.

Small cockles, limpets or cup shells may be used for pansy petals. Matching them up is the important thing.

For the pansies in Figure 5.15, we used cup shells that are listed in shell catalogs as "extra large." You can buy any color desired. This arrangement uses purple, orchid, orange, yellow, white and pink and is a good way to use up the two or three colors left over from flowers that take many shells of a single color. In this arrangement we made flowers with the two darkest petals at the top and the three lower petals of a lighter hue. However, you may want to vary this color choice, for of all flowers, the pansy holds the least true to a set coloring.

Since the pansy is almost flat, you may make it on your work sheet with a plastic disk, a bit of glue-soaked cotton, or in the case of small ones, with merely a puddle of glue.

First glue down the two top petals. Then glue the next two side shells slightly overlapping the top ones. Finally, glue on the round bottom shell. Place the rolled hinges facing toward the center. Now finish by touching up the center either with a bit of dark dye or paint or by gluing on a small limpet shell with a dark center or even by gluing on a cluster of black seeds. The dark center gives the flower that distinctive pansy look so much like that of a small face.

Your creativity can go wild in designing shell jewelry.
There is no end to the possibilities; almost every small shell
you have can be used in some way for jewelry.

Our heirloom, convex-glassed pictures are our pride and joy.

This tiny bouquet is only five inches high. The background is royal blue velure paper, the flowers are tiny cup shells and the leaves are dyed sea oats.

Fig. 5.15 We usually use only natural items in our shell creations, but for the pansy arrangement we thought the velvet leaves looked nice. We also cheated a little in painting the "faces" on the petal shells.

The pansy, like other flowers of this size, may be glued, when dry, to the coil end of a wire with a bit of cotton, or it may be glued directly to a background. The picture of the basket of pansies is a combination of the two (or may be called espaliered). We fastened each pansy to a wire coil and then glued them to a black velure background.

We were not satisfied using carp scales for pansy leaves because of their shape, so we experimented and came up with a fairly good effect using velvet leaves. Even so, we could not find leaves that looked exactly like those of the pansy, so we purchased some velvet grape leaves (which are quite large), cut them into three sections, making three leaves out of each one, and then shaped them to look as nearly like pansy leaves as we could. We glued the leaves to twists in the flower stems. Be sure to make the flower stems long enough to allow for the wire that is taken up with these twists and loops.

Clusters and Spikes

Clustered masses of tiny flowers and tall, graceful spikes add tremendously to a mixed bouquet. True, they are time-consuming and delicate work, but if carefully made, they are very lifelike.

The clusters (which include lilac, peony and snowball) are the hardest to make, so we'll discuss them first to get them behind us. There are several ways to make clusters. You may take the easiest way out—buy some plastic flowers, pull the blossoms from the stems, and after making all the individual shell flowers on your work sheet, glue them on the stems with bits of glue-soaked cotton.

Another way is to start from scratch, wiring each previously made flower with fine wire and then wiring these to a perforated plastic disk (see Fig. 5.3). Make all the individual flowers on your work sheet, and with a bit of gluey cotton, glue each one to a coil (see Fig. 5.16) on a two-inch piece of fine, 28 gauge, green wire. Push the wires of all the little individual flowers through the holes in the disk, pull them down to the stem wire and wrap them with florist tape (see Fig. 5.17). In order to give the cluster a rounded appearance, leave the center flowers standing taller on their wires and progressively pull the wires tighter toward the sides of the clump. Be sure the flowers are thick enough to cover the disk. It might be wise to paint the disk the color of the flowers to make sure it won't show.

For spikes or stalks, such as lupine, delphinium and hyacinth, we start with a long loop in a stem wire on which we have formed a spike of glue-soaked cotton that is tapered at the top (see Fig. 5.1). We have included step by step pictures of this method to explain it clearly. It is merely a matter

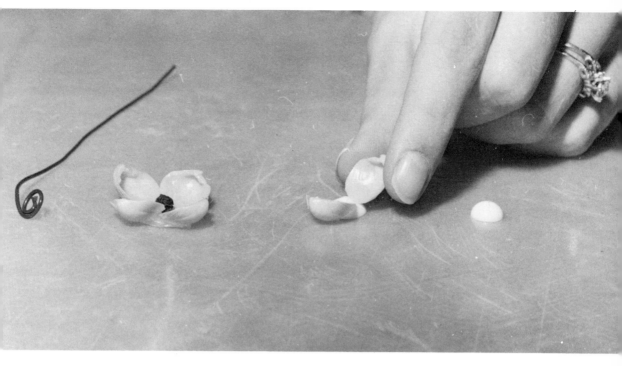

Fig. 5.16 The first step in making cluster flowers is to make all the individual flowers on your plastic work sheet. Begin with a puddle of glue, seat petals in it and add a center. When the glue is dry, glue the flowers to fine (28 gauge) wire stems.

Fig. 5.17 When all the individual flowers have been made, bunch them into a cluster and wrap the stems, as one, with green florist tape.

of choosing little shells, or tiny, previously made flowers, and gluing them around the spike of cotton until you have entirely covered it (see Fig. 5.18). Use the very smallest shells or flowers at the top. These will be the spurs that are not yet developed. In the example shown, a spike of lupine, we used coquina shells. For others, such as delphinium, make little individual flowers of four or five petals using rose cups and glue them close together on the spike. Make the flowers toward the top with three petals, so they look as though they have not yet opened. Real delphiniums are often seen in beautiful blue shades. These shell spikes, dyed a light blue, add contrast to a garden bouquet of mixed shell flowers.

For the finishing touch to all these spikes and clusters, wrap the stems right on up over the base with florist tape. If you are going to use leaves (plastic or fish scale), this is the time to wrap them in on the stem (see Fig. 5.19).

Sprays

Though we have already discussed making fruit blossoms, which are actually sprays, it might be well to add a bit. There are so many different kinds of sprays, some quite tiny, some like little droopy bells, and others, such as honeysuckle, so oddly shaped that we have not been able to duplicate them with shells. (If someone else has, we would love to hear about it.) Sprays are certainly not at all easy to make, but if works of art were simple, there would not be that great feeling of satisfaction in creating them.

Make the individual flowers for the drooping sprays on your work sheet. As with the clusters previously described, you may simply glue them to plastic stems from which the plastic flowers have been removed. To make your own stems, make the flowers and then glue each little individual flower to the coil of a 1½-inch piece of fine, 28 gauge, wire (see Fig. 5.20). After these dry, twist the wires together, staggering the flowers so that they are about ½ inch apart and drooping on about ½-inch stems. Of course, the size of the flowers determines the distance between them and the length of the stem; increase the distance and the length of the stem for larger flowers and decrease it for tiny ones, such as the lily of the valley (see Fig. 5.21). After the flowers are formed into a spray, twist them onto a larger stem wire. Hide the joint with a few leaves or with green florist tape. This is a delicate piece of work, but it is highly rewarding when you view the lovely, drooping spray of flowers you have created.

If the flowers are colored and the white gluey cotton at the base is too noticeable, you might want to paint the cotton the color of the flower or touch

Fig. 5.18 To make spikes of flowers, first form a tapered base of gluey cotton over a long loop of wire. Then, beginning at the top, glue small shells around in layers. We used coquinas for this one.

Fig. 5.19 To finish the spike, wrap florist tape around the stem and up over the cotton base. On this one we wrapped in a plastic leaf.

53

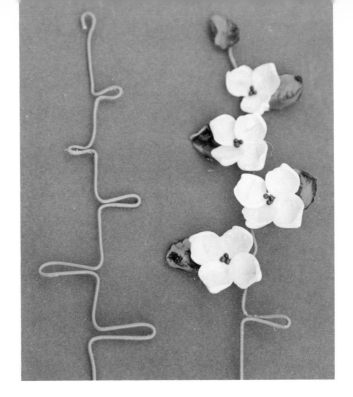

Fig. 5.20 Flower sprays can be made by gluing previously made flowers to twists of wire. If you wish to include fish scale leaves with the flowers, make the wire loops a little longer and glue a leaf under the outside edge of each flower.

Fig. 5.21 Sprays of tiny blossoms add greatly to the beauty of a bouquet. Here are two ways to make lily of the valley sprays. In the first, each flower is made with three tiny cup shells that are glued, with cotton, around loops in 21 gauge stem wire. The second is made of single snail shells that are glued to small loops on the stem wire.

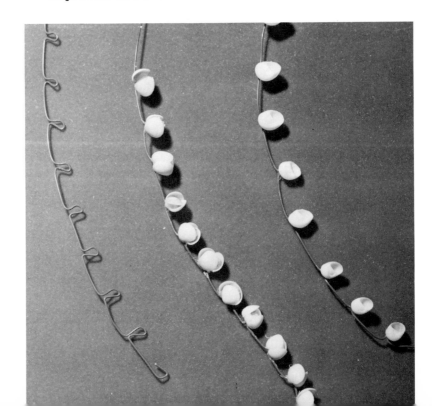

Fig. 5.22 These flower arrangements, made by the craftsmen at The Shell Factory near Ft. Myers, Florida, are large (from two- to four-foot) wall hangings.

it with green. For white flowers, leaving the base white should be all right.

The lily of the valley is typical of the drooping spray. These tricky little things can be faked by gluing barnacles directly to a stem, but they are much more realistic if each barnacle is glued to a tiny coil of fine wire and drooped along by twisting as described above. Another method is to twist loops in fine wire at intervals of from 1/3 to 1/2 inch (depending on the size of the shells) and glue the shells to the loops with a tiny bit of cotton.

For other drooping sprays, such as bleeding tooth, use either small olives or bubble shells. Study a picture of the spray you wish to make, study the shells you have on hand, and then choose those shells that most closely resemble the flowers. For all sprays, place the tiniest, more tightly closed flowers at the outer ends (see Figs. 5.22, 5.23 and Color Plates). 55

Fig. 5.23 White dogwood seemed ideally suited to decorate this great sea fan.

Other Flowers

Dozens of flowers can be made of shells, and one book could not contain specific instructions for each one. Use your imagination to dream up other blossoms. Isn't this, after all, the fun in creating works of art? Instruction is needed, of course, to learn the basic steps. Then too, through the many years that shell art has been practiced, craftsmen have learned which shells best form which flowers, and you can learn much from them. After copying a few of these, you will be able to study the shells you have on hand and see in them the possibilities for many other types of flowers. The above instructions are only basic suggestions to get you started.

Centers

The centers of flowers are as varied as the flowers themselves, sometimes even within the same species. When you branch out from the centers previously described with the individual flowers, it will take some research to determine the kind of center to use.

For many, such as the partially opened rose, you can build your petals around a wired univalve shell used as an unopened bud. You will have to study those that have wide-open centers, such as daisies and poppies, to learn what type of center to use. Is the center flat, is it a low, open circle, or is it made up of a close mat of short or tall stamens? Study the flower and decide; then choose the material that most nearly approximates its appearance.

A great variety of things may be used effectively for centers—yellow mustard seeds, black seeds of various sizes, tiny whelk shells, lilac shells, little rose cups, barnacles, and even such spices as whole cloves and peppercorns. You can purchase materials to make centers at the grocery store or at hobby shops that carry flower-making or shellcraft materials. Clusters of stamens are available at hobby shops in many colors and materials. We experimented with some that looked like tiny pearls extended on yellow stems and found their appearance quite pleasing.

However, preferring to compose our flowers as much as possible from treasures provided by the sea, we constantly search for items that might be used for centers. Often, as we roam the beaches, we come upon the big coil of a whelk's egg sack that has been cast up on the sand and has dried out. Sometimes the whelks in these are undeveloped, but we often find in them hundreds of perfectly formed baby whelks that were probably on the verge of hatching when they were cast from the sea. If the meat has not completely dried, they may be a little odorous and will need to be dried and soaked in bleach. These make excellent centers when used in clusters; for tiny flowers, they may be used singly. The whelks and other small univalves may be glued with either the points or open ends up, depending on the type of center required.

Other tiny shells which are ideal for centers may be found by scooping up the shell-filled sand of the beach drifts at the edge of the waves and sorting through it.

Centers that bulge up in the middle may be built up with glue-soaked cotton; those that are flat (e.g., pansies) may have a round shell or operculum glued flat, or they may simply be painted on.

Many flowers, such as some dahlias and zinnias, have no apparent centers. Their centers are merely petals, tinier and more deeply colored than those on the outer edges.

Buds

Flower buds, like centers, vary greatly according to the type of flower. The rose and other flowers of this type may have a tightly closed bud. For these a conical-shaped univalve of the proper size and color is excellent. A small conch shell or a paper-thin whelk looks exactly like a rosebud with its petals only just beginning to unfurl.

To wire univalve shells for buds, drill a hole in the closed end, push a stem wire up in the hole and bond it with some glue-soaked cotton. When the glue is dry, an artificial calyx or one made by cutting points from green florist tape may be glued around the base of the bud. In the case of some types of flowers, there is no calyx; for these, tape may be wrapped over the base.

A cluster of buds will add realism to an arrangement of cluster and spray flowers; seldom do all the flowers on a plant bloom at the same time. Variety may be introduced with partly opened buds as well as tightly closed ones. Use a wired (or for small ones, unwired) univalve for the centers of partly opened buds and glue on three or four petals, lapping them closely around it.

Tiny bubble shells, augers, or even pairs of coquinas, fitted together, may serve as buds for very small flowers. In one flat picture arrangement of seeds and shells, we made buds with a small auger for the center and two coquinas at the sides as though they were just beginning to open up. We glued these buds to the background of the picture along the stems of a sea fern, and the arrangement was most interesting.

Foliage

Flower foliage varies so greatly with the different species that here too it is wise to study pictures of the flower you are making to determine what foliage to use. We found when we began making shell flowers that, except for a few, we had no idea what kind of foliage the different kinds of flowers had. It took some research to make each of them.

However, you don't have to use any leaves on the stems. You could take a cue from arrangers in flower shops and use, interspersed among the flowers, foliage not even related to the flowers themselves. Florists use ferns, ti leaves, huckleberry and even dried baby's breath and other delicate or glossy fill-in foliage. Plastic versions may be used with your shell flowers. Of course you should choose foliage proportionate to that of the flowers. You would not, for instance, use the great coarse ti leaves or large philodendron with an arrange-
58 ment of small flowers.

If you are a purist and want every component in your arrangement to come from the sea, you may either buy green-dyed shells of various types from your shellcraft supplier or dye them yourself. Big, flat scallops, dyed green, make excellent pond lily pads; green-dyed coquinas and other elongated shells make leaves for medium-sized flowers; for the leaves of small flowers, such as those to be used in miniature arrangements and for jewelry, we purchase small green-dyed gar scales shaped exactly like the leaves of a rose. These scales are often thick and have a shell-like quality. They make nice leaves for small flowers, but for larger and free-standing flowers we prefer the more delicate carp scales.

The simplest way to provide foliage for shell flowers is to buy plastic or cloth leaves at the flower-making department of your hobby shop; but the purist will want fish scales. Some craft shops sell these scales by the pint. Sometimes dyed scales can be found, and you can usually get them in exactly the hue desired.

Several kinds of fish have large scales suitable for leaves, and since most of these are food fish caught by commercial fishermen, we need have no guilt feelings about using them. The gar, carp and buffalo (freshwater fish) and the mullet and redfish (saltwater fish) all have good "leaf" scales. You can buy these at some shops. Tarpon also have excellent scales for leaves—huge ones, in some cases, but these cannot be legally sold. You have to be a fisherman or have a friend who is a fisherman to obtain these. One excellent way to get a large amount of scales is to haunt the places where commercial fishermen are cleaning their catch. They have no use for the scales and usually have no objection to your collecting them.

Fresh scales require some preparation. They have to be washed and rinsed with bleach and water. Partially dry them before dyeing by spreading the scales out on sheets of paper toweling with another layer of toweling on top. Some scales curl badly if not weighted with a board while drying.

Use warm, not boiling, dye; very hot water deteriorates scales. Experiment with mixtures to attain a color that pleases you. If the green seems too much on the blue side, add a little yellow; if it is too bright to look leaflike, add a bit of red dye—red and green are opposite on the color scale and will neutralize each other when mixed. Mixed in equal parts, red and green make a perfect grey, so don't add too much red.

Remove a scale from the dye bath occasionally to judge its shade. When the proper shade has been attained, remove the scales, and rinse and spread them out on paper toweling. More complete directions can be found in Chapter 3.

Fish scales may be used in flat arrangements, on the stems of flowers, or on leafy twigs. For flat arrangements, simply glue the scales to the back- 59 ground at intervals, as though they were on stems or space them along the stems of flowers in the arrangement. For use in other kinds of arrangements, glue the scales on fine wire in which loops have been twisted. Arrange these in sprays of three or five, and then use florist tape to wrap them at intervals along the stems of flowers.

Sprays or branches of fish scale leaves, interspersed among the flowers, are almost as effective. To make these, twist loops in a stem wire—small loops near the top and larger loops as you go down. Glue your smallest scales at the top and larger ones as you go down the stem. Number 21 gauge wire is fine for fastening leaves to the flower stem, and either 21 or 18 is good for the twigs (see Fig. 5.24).

Obviously, all flowers do not have the same kind of leaves. When you make leaves for a certain variety of flower, try to duplicate those peculiar to that flower, even to the point of shaping the scales with scissors. Remember that sprays of leaves are usually shaped like an elongated pyramid, with each stem point bearing a leaf, regardless of the number along its length.

Tiny scales may be made into ferns by wiring them on very fine wire, a delicate operation. The directions for making sprays of flowers can be applied to these scale ferns. They add beauty to a bouquet and may be bent gracefully and arranged among the flowers at the sides of a bouquet.

Spraying fish scale leaves with lacquer or varnish prevents any fading of their colors and strengthens them. Whether you use glossy or nongloss lacquer is a matter of choice.

Fig. 5.25 This bouquet was made totally of shells, with the exception of the fish-scale
poppies in the upper midsection and the green-dyed fish-scale leaves.

Flower Basket

The mixed bouquet pictured in Figure 5.25 (see Color Plates) is made
up of a wide variety of flowers that were created with shells and fish scales.
This bouquet indicates the many types of shell flowers that can be copied from
the real thing. Single blossoms, clusters, spikes, sprays and woody tree
branches, all appear.

61

Fig. 5.24 To make carp, gar, mullet, buffalo or redfish scale leaves, make loops in 18
or 21 gauge green-coated wire and glue the dyed scales to the loops.

All the flowers pictured here were made of shells except the deep yellow, rose and white poppies; these are dyed carp scales. The purist would be delighted with this bouquet. No artificial foliage has been used except for the calyxes of the rosebuds. All the leaves are dyed fish scales.

We used more than a dozen different kinds of shells for the flowers in this bouquet.

Dogwood shells (or Florida lucinas) for the branch of white dogwood on the left.

Cup shells (both dyed and in the natural white and light pink) for most of the sprays and clusters and some of the single roses.

Pearly clams for the large magnolia in the lower center.

Jingle shells in natural shades of orange and yellow for the large flowers near the center.

Coquinas in natural colors for the spikes of lupines and the zinnias and dahlias.

Fluted conchs, painted with pearl essence, for the cluster of buds at the lower left.

Slipper shells in natural pinkish white for the flower in the upper center.

Pearl snails about ¼ inch wide for the sprays of tiny lily of the valley, at the outer edge.

Large carp scales for the rose, white, and deep yellow poppies.

The sprays of leaves are all dyed carp scales. The centers are peppercorns, yellow mustard seeds, black seeds, cloves, lilac shells, rice shells and other tiny shells of various kinds.

6

Arrangements

Now that the general basics of making individual flowers have been mastered, let's get on with the arranging. The possibilities here are endless. Those flowers that have been wired may be used in free-standing bouquets in vases, pots, urns or large shells. They may even be arranged in a spray on a piece of driftwood—a most interesting way to display shell flowers. Large magnolias and lotus may be wired in sprays with leaves and buds to form gorgeous wall plaques. We saw one such arrangement, made of many large flowers and formed in an attractive S curve, that was almost six feet long!

Shell flowers have even more possibilities for arranging than do fresh flowers; with the elimination of the need for a water container, there comes a freedom of choice. Size is not a factor for you can create a six-foot spray of large lotus; a free-standing conventional bouquet; a spray of dogwood under a glass dome (see Color Plates); an apple blossom sprig draped on a piece of twisted driftwood; a tiny miniature bouquet in a shadow-boxed gold filigree frame (see Color Plates); or a wreath of small shell flowers encircling the glass of an oval mirror or a picture frame. Many such shell creations are hundreds of years old and still absolutely lovely!

Some kinds of flowers lend themselves nicely to mixed bouquets, and others seem shown off to their best advantage when displayed alone. A branch of white shell dogwood blossoms in a heavenly blue vase is a gorgeous sight; a miniature bouquet made of tiny shell rosebuds of a delicate pink shade is adorable.

When arranging your flowers, follow the few general rules laid down by those experienced in the art, and then give your imagination free rein and go on to create your own masterpiece.

When a container is used, you must first fill it with green florist clay or Styrofoam® cut to fit. Use the sticky clay sold by florists to hold·the Styrofoam firmly in the container. Seat the heavier, larger arrangements firmly to counter any top-heavy effect.

It is a good idea to decide prior to making your flowers just how they are to be used. Then you can be sure to make the stems the right length, to turn the flower faces in the right direction (as in the case of those that are to be glued directly to the background), and to make the proper number of flowers. Get the container set up and ready, with the Styrofoam seated, and as the flowers are finished, push their stems down into the foam and study the effect. After a few flowers are seated, it is easy to see how many more, what sizes and what shapes are needed. For instance, if at one point an arrangement of straight-standing posies looks far too stiff, soften the lines with curved sprays at the sides. Then step back and study it again. Perhaps it's still too rounded. In that case, make several tall spikes of delphinium and stand them in graduated heights near the back center. That's better still. But one more addition is needed; a spray of white fruit blossoms at an angle across the lower front.

The type of container is a matter of choice but an unadorned, plain-colored or white one is best; an ornate container is likely to detract from the flowers. A short bowl is effective for some arrangements, a tall vase for others. Feel it out for yourself; not everyone likes the same thing.

However, whether arranging real or artificial flowers, it is a good general rule to have the tallest of the flowers stand about 1½ times as high as the container. Arranging shell flowers follows the same general plan as arranging real flowers. The sprays, spikes and buds usually either stand tallest or are located on the outer edges. Since your flowers have wire stems, they can be bent in graceful curves. Leave the middle stems straight with some draping or drooping singles or side sprays. The larger flowers should be placed toward the middle or slightly off-center rather than at the outer edges or top.

Your foliage (see Chapter 5) can be of artificial ferns or leaves of plastic, dyed fish scale sprays, or such things as sea fans and sea whips.

A large, snowy whelk shell or horse conch makes a lovely container for crescent-shaped arrangements. These many-footed shells seem created purposely for display. Turned one way they stand with point up, forming a deep cup; shifted to another position, the cup faces toward the front with the shell lying almost horizontal. Either position is attractive. The final choice depends on the stem length and the number of flowers used, so here again try the arrangement in different ways until you find the way that pleases you.

Fig. 6.1 This attractive wall hanging of driftwood and shell flowers was created by Margaret Elgersman. The leaves in this arrangement are made of univalve operculums (trapdoors).

Driftwood complements shell flowers beautifully (see Fig. 6.1). Wire the flowers into a spray. Then either lay or wire the spray onto the curve of the driftwood or insert it into holes drilled in the wood. These combination driftwood-floral arrangements are lovely either free-standing or when used as wall plaques. Driftwood also sets off displayed shells (see Fig. 6.2). Spraying the wood with lacquer or low-gloss varnish helps it to shed dust. Better yet, spray the entire arrangement once it is completed. The lacquer allows the arrangement to be washed when it gets dirty and it helps to retain colors.

Shadow Boxes and Convex-Glassed Frames

Since shell pictures are three-dimensional, they may be beautifully displayed in shadow boxes from two to six inches in depth. This method has the great advantage of protecting the picture from dust and dirt. Glassed shadow

Fig. 6.2 A background of driftwood sets off the Mao's large horse conch to good advantage.

boxes and frames containing different kinds of shell arrangements have survived the rigors of hundreds of years to become treasured collectors' items now seen in museums.

Anyone who is handy with a saw can take an ordinary picture frame and build a box on the back of it. You may want to paint the inside of the box, but we like to cover it with black velvet or some other shade or type of cloth that shows off the shells and their colors to good advantage. Large and deep shadow box frames can be wired for a small showcase bulb to light the picture.

With shadow boxes and convex-glassed frames, flowers can be arranged in two different manners: if the frame is medium to deep, they may be wired and seated in a narrow container (see Fig. 6.3); for more shallow frames, they may be glued directly to the background. If you are creating an arrangement in a shallow frame you can place those flowers that stand out most toward the center in order to give a rounded effect (see Figs. 6.4, 6.5 and Color Plates).

Ferns and other greenery, splayed out on the background or with their lower stems glued partially under the flowers, make pleasing foliage. As in free-standing arrangements it is a good idea to have the larger flowers in the middle or lower, off-center regions.

If you use a container, fill it with Styrofoam or florist clay and plant the stems in the same way as in free-standing bouquets. The only difference is

Fig. 6.3 We lined this shadow box with red velure paper purchased at an art supply shop. The delicate little sprays of flowers are made of small rose cups and the leaves are green-dyed carp scales. All are made on 21 gauge, green-coated wire.

Fig. 6.4 The convex glass of our oval antique frames did not always afford the desired depth for our floral arrangements. My husband Ray solved this problem by building oval, velvet-lined shadow boxes for them.

Fig. 6.5 The flowers in this (and our other) oval frame are mostly free standing, but a few are glued to the velvet.

that since the arrangements are one-sided, most of the flowers face the front or have turned-up faces. For picture frames with curved glass, you must, of course, have the deepest part of the arrangement to the center.

One ancient but still lovely convex-glassed frame that we saw in a museum was lined with black velvet. It contained a spray of wild roses arranged in a graceful curve, without a container. The roses were so real and fresh looking that they seemed only recently cut. Another such frame, of more recent making, held a branch of manzanita on which a mass of snowy pear blossoms was growing. Branches of the little western mountain manzanita tree can be purchased at florists. They serve nicely for woody flowering plants, such as dogwood or apple blossoms.

It is not absolutely necessary to glass over shadow boxes and frames made to hang on the wall (though it is desirable). If the background and flowers are sprayed with lacquer, they will be washable, but you would not want to spray or wash a velvet background. You may use a conventional frame without a shadow box for an unglassed picture, but the three-dimensional effect will be partially lost.

Coffee and End Table Shadow Boxes

If someone in your family is handy with tools, you might consider making a shadow-boxed coffee table that can be used for a seascape, for a floral arrangement, or as a showcase for your shell collection (see Fig. 6.6). Any table can be converted. The shadow box is made the same size as the table and of the same or contrasting wood. It is then placed on top of the table and attached with hinges or simply made to lift off completely. Either heavy, strong glass or a sheet of Plexiglas® or other plastic is used for the top. Shell mosaics are nice displayed this way. Looking down at them, as you sit, you are able to study the intricate designs at your leisure.

One of our favorite shell flower arrangements is actually no arrangement at all but simply a beautiful, rose-colored pond lily wired with one bud and green scallop lily pads (see Fig. 6.7). A friend displays a coral-colored lily of this type on a stemmed silver server, and another has a single big white magnolia blossom (made of macomas) on a stemmed bonbon dish made of rich, dark red crystal.

Lamps and Night Lights

Many shells have a translucent quality; a light placed in back of them creates a lovely, opalescent glow, and this makes them admirably suited for 69 lamps. We experimented with several types of shells for wall lights and night lights and came up with some quite interesting ideas.

A basket made of a large, colorful scallop shell (the baking shells that are sold in sets of four or six are fine for this) and glued to a base made of a sun ray venus or some other shallow shell with a small roll of gluey cotton makes a good little night light. We planted ours with shell flowers and some real cured ferns (see Fig. 6.8). We backed this with a deeply cupped cockle-shell and bored a hole in the cockle so that we could insert a cord and install a small light bulb.

You can make shades for wall lights by wiring large scallop shells with a fastener that fits around the bulb or bulb base (see Fig. 6.9). This shade may be left undecorated or may be trimmed with shell designs or shell flowers.

Containers and Arrangers

We have already discussed briefly some types of containers and arrangers we like to use, in the flower arranging section of this chapter, but perhaps a

Fig. 6.6 A shadow-boxed coffee table makes an interesting display cabinet for favorite shells and other sea creatures. We saw this one at a shell show. *Courtesy of Bette O. Parke*

Fig. 6.7 A rose-colored pond lily makes a nice centerpiece.

Fig. 6.8 The possibilities for night lights are many—just use your imagination. Here are three examples. The palm tree fronds in the nativity scene are made of large gar scales.

Fig. 6.9 This lampshade is made of one large white scallop shell. Installed on a wall of the Mao's home, it casts a soft, translucent light over the room.

more detailed discussion is called for here. Then too, there are so many types available, if you know where to look for them, and we don't want to overlook any possibilities.

For example (again for the purist, who strives for arrangements consisting only of shells), what could be more apropos for a container than a large white whelk shell, a pearly pink queen conch, or a brilliant red horse conch. All of these are knobbed in such a way as to provide a firm footing at several different angles, and if the angle does not quite suit, you may grind off one of the feet until it does.

We found the huge snow-white whelk shown in Figure 5.12 while floating in our canoe on St. Joseph's Bay, on the northern curve of the Gulf of Mexico. We were in shallow water only a short distance out from the campground of the T. H. Stone Memorial Park. This was a delightful discovery: it was the largest and most perfect whelk we had ever found. Surprisingly, it did not contain a live animal. It has often been our experience to find large, completely undamaged and yet tenantless shells in these calm, protected bays of the Gulf, and we attribute this to the fact that the animals probably came in to lay their eggs and died there. Because of the mild wave action, the shells have not been subjected to the rolling, tumbling action of the heavier surf, which causes erosion and breakage. The fact that we see a great many of the large egg case coils of the whelk in these bays confirms our theory.

Whatever color it may be, a large shell makes an excellent container for displaying shell flowers. For that matter, a deeply cupped whelk or conch can also be used as a container for fresh-cut flowers or as a planter, with the only requirement being a cavity large enough to contain water or soil.

But while we are discussing the great single univalves for arrangers, let's not overlook the other treasures the sea has to offer. There is, for instance, the coral cluster. Those millions of infinitesimal creatures that make up a cluster of coral are artists in their own right, and the remarkable formations of coral are often so very attractive that they can be displayed alone, as a base for a flower arrangement, or with a variety of other sea creatures.

A friend of ours, a Mrs. Lamb who lives on an island off the Florida coast, has a huge, magnificent cluster of gleaming white coral gracing her dining table at all times. Each time we are invited to the Lambs' home, we look forward not only to the pleasure it gives us to be with these gracious people, but with a lively anticipation of seeing the centerpiece Mrs. Lamb will have arranged for the affair. It is never the same, though the great coral forest always forms the basis for the design. Sometimes, interspersed among the coral branches, there will be large, red hibiscus blossoms, and at another time it has taken on the appearance of an undersea scene, with brilliantly colored shells and sea creatures among its branches.

As we have said previously, another excellent arranger may be formed of an unusual piece of driftwood. But let's carry the idea further and say that just any old driftwood will not do—there should be something unique about it. Strangely gnarled and twisted pieces can of course be purchased at roadside shops that cater to tourists; but, though it is more difficult to find attractive pieces, it is much more fun to find your own. But where do we look? It is easy to miss the driftwood while beachcombing; since it is lightweight, it is often carried by waves far up on the beach, perhaps caught in the exposed roots of trees or back of sand mounds.

To carry out the idea of using natural rather than manufactured containers, one of our friends cut a coconut in half, sawing scallops in the edge. Three snail shell feet were glued on for a base, and a bouquet composed of coconut "wood roses" and shell flowers was arranged in the shell. Another 73

Fig. 6.10   Three, medium-sized whelk shells, planted with shell and fish-scale flowers, make lovely hanging baskets. We drilled holes in each shell and hung them on gold-colored chains of varying lengths.

friend fastened a pearly nautilus shell like a cornucopia on a piece of gnarled driftwood and planted a spray of shell peach blossoms in it. And still another (whose hobbies include ceramics), finding it difficult to get vases and pots narrow enough to fit into shadow boxes, made bisque half-pots for them by blocking off a section of her mold when she poured the ceramic slip.

Hanging Baskets

New and different decorative items are often dreamed up as a result of incidents that occur. The idea for our hanging basket whelk evolved literally from a series of accidents; after it had been knocked from a table several times, we turned it into a hanging basket for preservation.

74

Fig. 6.11 Phillis Anderson's citronella shell-candle.

At first, for a hanger, we used a chain made of reed links. This was rather nice, but we decided that the links were too large to show off the shell to best advantage and that they even detracted from its beauty. We finally settled on a gold-colored chain that we purchased at a hobby shop. We drilled two holes in the shell. Fastening two lengths of chain in them with small gold rings, we brought the chains together and fastened them to a single chain. This completed our hanging basket.

Now what to use it for? In another room there was a wall vase containing some rather odd plastic flowers that we had never really liked. We pulled off the plastic flowers, glued on some shell flowers and presto! We had a pleasant basket of flowers (see Fig. 6.10).

Queen conchs, nautiluses, large ruffled clams and other large shells can also be used for hanging baskets. We like a draped appearance for hanging basket flowers, but this is not necessary. A mixed bouquet, or even a large single flower with fish-scale leaves can also be nice.

A shell that is not in good enough condition to be displayed can be used in other ways. Our friend, Phillis Anderson, filled one such shell with citronella candle wax, added two wicks, made a macrame hanger and hung the shell-candle outside to discourage mosquitoes. The light shining through the red-dyed wax and shell gave the whole a rosy glow (see Fig. 6.11).

Panel Displays

To make a panel display you may use corkboard or the rough side of a rectangle of Masonite®. We prefer the corkboard, even though it has the disadvantage of being rather crumbly and really needs a stiff backing (see Fig. 6.12).

For the panel pictured in Figure 6.13, we used a corkboard three feet long and one foot wide and glued a matching piece of 3/16-inch pegboard to the back. A board with holes is used because some of the heavier items cannot be held by glue alone and need to be wired. Holes in the Masonite are handy for the wiring.

Before gluing the corkboard to the Masonite, loop a strong wire through two of the holes about eight inches down from the top of the Masonite. Twist the ends together at the back for a hanger and then glue the two boards together. Now you are ready to arrange your treasures from the sea.

Before fastening them on, lay them in various patterns on the board and study your arrangements to obtain the most pleasing effect. Then, when you have decided on a pattern, remove the smaller items (it is easier to glue them on later) and, lifting the larger ones one at a time, mark their locations in chalk.

Install a wire across the back of each of the larger items, such as the big starfish, boring holes in the star where needed. Then, punching two holes from back to front through the soft corkboard, wire each of the larger items in place.

Now the arrangement can again be studied and the smaller items moved around for best effect before gluing. Don't forget that here too gluey cotton can be used as a bonding agent between board and shells. It may even be strong enough to hold your larger items if they are not exceptionally heavy.

Now the display is finished except for the lacquer spray. This is a matter of choice. We sprayed the pictured panel (see Fig. 6.13) rather thoroughly with a clear, low-gloss varnish and found that it helped to firm up the corkboard and make it less crumbly.

76

Fig. 6.12 Corkboard is excellent for a panel display, but it is wise to back it with a piece of pegboard of the same size to strengthen it. The holes in the pegboard simplify wiring.

Fig. 6.13 Don't forget that many items besides shells may be found while beachcombing. Most of the things displayed on this corkboard panel were found on Gulf of Mexico beaches.

77

Fig. 6.14 A colorful whelk planted with carp-scale or shell flowers and fastened in a deep frame makes an unusual, three-dimensional picture.

We chose some of our larger, more interesting finds for our panel display and used quite a number of items that could not be used in floral arrangements or smaller beach and sea scenes. We have used sea fans, sea whips, and the large starfish to tie our picture together, but in your wanderings, you may have found an especially interesting twisty piece of driftwood or some very large shell that would serve the same purpose.

We really wanted to frame our panel with an edging of thick rope aged in seawater. We have decided to leave our panel unframed until we locate the kind of rope we want; right now it does not have quite the nautical effect we wanted to achieve.

Finding Frames

You can frame your displays with anything. As we just mentioned, an aged rope might give a nautical effect. Ornate gold filigree adds an heirloom-like quality. A deep frame (see Fig. 6.14) containing your most colorful whelk planted with carp-scale or shell flowers presents an unusual, three-dimensional effect. One of the loveliest ways to show off your three-dimensional floral arrangement is in an oval frame covered with convex glass—but just try to find one! Deciding that we just must have one oval frame, we set out on a frame-hunting safari quite confident that every used furniture store would have them sitting around by the dozens to be had practically for the asking. After all, weren't these frames quite common in great-grandpa's day? Every home had a wedding portrait of great-grandpa and great-grandma sitting in stiff dignity in an oval, convex-glassed frame on one wall of the parlor and a similar frame displaying a picture of the United States Capitol on the other wall.

We sallied forth merrily on our safari; we returned utterly defeated! Oh, we found some ancient frames—each secondhand store had two or three —but the prices were outrageous. The frames were no longer placed in the secondhand category, but had attained that impressive title "antique" and were thus objects far too rich for us.

Then why, we asked ourselves, must we have the convex glass? That glass is probably what makes the frame so expensive. We will, then, just get an old oval frame for our flowers and leave it unglassed.

Again we girded ourselves, took up sword and charged off to the battle-field. After many hard-fought dealings, we wound up with one prize at such cost that its purchase entailed something close to taking out a lifetime mortgage on the house to buy it! Lucky are those shell artists whose ancestors were hoarders, for their attics are treasure troves of frames.

79

But even at the cost, we felt the purchase was worthwhile; there is something about an oval frame that sets a floral arrangement off to its best advantage, and we consider the resultant picture (see Color Plates) to be an heirloom that will be handed down through the generations of our family. We sprayed all the flowers with a low-gloss lacquer and are hoping they will stay fairly clean—with the glass, we would not have had this worry.

However, this is not the end of the story of our hunt for convex-glassed frames. Later, when we had almost given up, we found two lovely ones miraculously within our price range. The floral arrangements in these (see Figs. 6.4 and 6.5) we consider to be our masterpieces. These were a dual effort; my husband, Ray, built them into deeper shadow boxes—not an easy task for oval frames!

When frames of this sort are made into deeper shadow boxes, it is possible to make the bouquet free-standing in a foam-filled container or partly free-standing with some of the flowers glued or wired to the background.

Here you will be confronted with a problem: a container shallow enough to fit the box is not easy to find. We managed to find a pair of gold-colored wall vases, in which we planted the flowers in our oval arrangements. If your hobbies include ceramics, you might fire your own container, using only half of the form of a vase. White bisque is lovely for these.

For a convex-glassed frame that does not have a shadow box, you may form the arrangement in a spray without a container, or you may want to use a large white scallop shell which is shallow enough to fit. With its ridged, fan shape, the scallop looks very much like a basket. As with the other type of container, the cup side should be filled with florist clay or Styrofoam to hold the stems of the flowers and foliage.

The beautiful shell art pictured here was shown at the famous Sanibel and Ft. Myers Shell Shows in Florida. Most of these items were either award winners or entered in the noncompetitive category. By studying Figures 6.15–6.21, you can get a good idea of the effects of various frames.

A large, colorful wall decoration made of shaded orange shells.

The blue flowers of this wall decoration have been carefully shaded to give them a natural look.

A basket filled with a wide variety of flowers is especially pretty. The shapes, colors and sizes of shells are so varied that almost any flower can be duplicated.

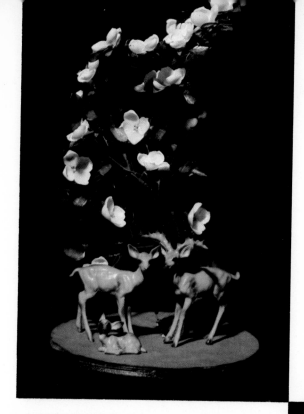

A tree of shell flowers with a sea whip trunk shelters this family of deer.

This lovely pond lily centerpiece was spray painted with a flat paint. Shading adds to the natural look.

Spray paint can color coral and shells beautifully, as evidenced by this floral arrangement made by the craftsmen of The Shell Factory, near Ft. Myers, Florida.

The possible shell designs for trimming hats and bags are many and varied.

Fig. 6.15 This lovely shell wreath, owned by Mr. and Mrs. George Greene, was made by Elizabeth Prall in the 1870s.

Fig. 6.16 One of the most beautiful forms of shell art is that of the shadow-boxed "Sailor's Valentine." Sailors made these for their sweethearts and mothers during the long days at sea. Helene Krupcik's valentine is the loveliest we have ever seen.

81

Fig. 6.17 Esther Rossitto's lilac bouquet looks amazingly real.

Fig. 6.18 These delicate flowers and foliage were made entirely of fishbones by Emma Guthrie.

Fig. 6.19 These three framed shell pictures, beautifully displayed on easels, were also made by Emma Guthrie.

Fig. 6.20 A large owl, with the most feathery feathers imaginable, was exhibited by E. J. Vegliante. It was made entirely of tarpon scales!

84

Fig. 6.21 A mixture of shells, driftwood and sea creatures went into the making of this unique picture by Bernadene Jerz.

7

Critters and Dolls

Each critter you make becomes an individual character in its own right. Since no two shells are alike, no two animals or birds made from shells will look the same (see Figs. 7.1–7.4). Of two shell pelicans, one will have its head held in a coy manner and is obviously a shy little girl pelican; another takes on a jaunty man about town air and is given a swanky slipper shell hat with a cocky feather (see Fig. 7.5). You decide as you work, and this is the real fun of making shell critters.

Choose your shells for critters in the same way—allow the appearance of the shell to suggest its purpose and then add the needed components. As you beachcomb, you will come upon a certain shell that, when you hold it up and study it, will suggest in your mind some part of an animal or bird. This idea will set you off on a hunt for other parts of the proper size and shape to go with it. Don't be bound by animal forms. With a little imagination shells will also suggest dolls and ships (see Fig. 7.6).

Pelican

For an example, we will take the pelican (the shells needed for him are quite plentiful) and go through the steps of creation from beginning to completion. You come upon a medium-sized whelk shell which looks like the comical, chunky little body of a pelican. Okay, then hunt for another smaller

Fig. 7.1 A wide variety of shells was used in making these critters, including limpets, conchs, cowries, cockles, augers, lucina, pearl clams, scallops, rice shells, whelks, rose cups, coquinas and squilla claws.

Fig. 7.2 A group of appealing tiny critters made mostly of cowries and coquinas. The body of the turtle on the left is a limpet shell.

Fig. 7.3 This assortment of small critters made by Margaret Elgersman contains some of the cleverest we have ever seen. The feathers of most of the birds are made of gar scales (natural white and dyed) and squilla claws. The bodies of the owls are sections of large pine cones, their ears are shark's teeth, their wings are coquins, and their feet are whelks. Backed with magnets, all adhere to metal.

Fig. 7.4 These ducks have matching pairs of turkey wing shells for bodies, snails for heads, either augers or coquinas for bills and coquinas for feet.

Fig. 7.5 It's fun to make these clever little characters. Obviously the fellow with the feather in his hat is a boy and the shy, bonneted one (flowers on the bonnet are barnacles) a girl. We purposely included this photo before correcting a mistake we had made in gluing: too much cotton bonding. The cotton shows where the body joins the feet.

Fig. 7.6 Boys love to make this sailing ship. It is not necessary to have these exact shells—similar ones will work as well.

89

whelk, fit it on the tip of the first and immediately you can see the pelican taking form. Now find some feet of the right size. These can be made of several different kinds of shells. Kitten's paws, slipper shells, jewel boxes, or even small oyster shells may serve. They should curve in opposite directions in order to have a right and left foot.

Now you have the main components for a pelican, but what about embellishments? Well if this one appears to have feminine characteristics, make her a girl bird and adorn her with an Easter bonnet or flowers on her head. All along the beach you will see small bivalves incrusted with barnacles, and it takes little imagination to picture the cupped shell as a bonnet and the barnacles as flower trimming. Try several of these on the pelican head and choose the one that fits best. Now, with the addition of some of those clever little rolling eyes sold in hobby shops (or eyes painted on), you have your pelican.

To assemble—wrap a small wad of glue-soaked cotton around the tip of the "body" whelk, fit the "head" whelk on at an interesting angle and allow it to dry (see Fig. 7.7). The feet are now glued on with a bit of cotton. Note that one picture we have included (Fig. 7.5) has a pelican with his feet improperly glued on (the cotton is too obvious). In shellcraft, gluey cotton is a must, but too much of it ruins the effect. Use only as much as is actually needed to bond the shells together. Now glue on (or paint) the eyes, and with the addition of a hat or a cluster of previously made flowers, your critter has become an individual personality (see Fig. 7.8).

Heron

For this bird use two matching cockles for the body, a wentletrap or auger for the bill, two coquinas for the head, kitten's paws for the feet and some large-sized pipe cleaners or chenille wire for the legs and neck.

First glue the two cockles together with glue-soaked cotton (the hinge parts will be at the joining of the neck). At the same time, glue the pipe cleaner legs and neck in between the cockles (see Fig. 7.9). Allow this to dry and then bend about one-third of the ends of the pipe cleaner legs out to form a base on which to glue the feet.

With the headless bird standing on its own two feet, it is easy to attach the auger or wentletrap head. If it is a small bird and the hole in the shell is not too large, apply glue to the end of the pipe cleaner neck and push it into the hole. If this does not hold, fill the hole with glue-soaked cotton.

Now study the heron. If he suits you as is, call it a day, but if the head seems too small, you can improve its shape by gluing two coquinas to the sides. Glue on small rolling eyes, and the critter is finished (see Fig. 7.10).

Mouse

This is the cute little fellow you see attached with his magnet tummy to refrigerators and other metal surfaces. The materials needed for a mouse are: one slipper shell for a body, two tiny rose cups for surprisingly realistic ears, three little black seeds for a nose and eyes, a rubber band for a tail and a small piece of magnet. The magnets come in coiled strips and can be cut to the desired size.

With a pair of scissors taper a 1½-inch piece of rubber band to resemble a mouse tail and cut a ½-inch piece from the coil of the magnet. Now fill the

Fig. 7.7 To make a pelican, choose a large whelk shell for the body and a smaller one for the head. Wrap a pad of gluey cotton around the "neck" and glue on the head. Now, with wisps of gluey cotton, glue on the feet. The feet may be made of slipper shells, small cockles, or other similar shells.

Fig. 7.8 Pam Jones completed her pelican by adding rolling eyes (these may be found at any hobby shop) and dressing it in a flowered Easter hat.

Fig. 7.9 For a comical looking heron, form two chenille wires into a circle and legs and neck, glue two matching cockles together (with the circle of chenille wire forming the bond) and then glue on a head and feet.

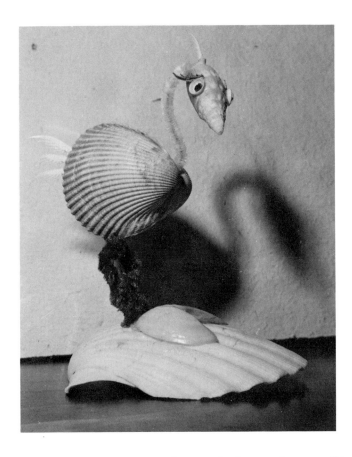

Fig. 7.10 For the final touches on the heron, glue on rolling eyes and a silly tail, topknot, and eyebrows of squilla claws. We call him Groucho.

cavity of the slipper shell with glue-soaked cotton and embed the end of the tail in it. Then, making sure you have the magnetic side of the magnet out, embed it in the cotton. Turn the mouse over, and with a toothpick, put two spots of glue on the shell in the proper places for eyes. Glue on your two smallest seeds for these and a slightly larger seed for the nose. The ears come next. Apply two spots of glue at the sides and back of the eyes. Seat the rose cups upright, cupped side forward.

These, as well as all the other animals and birds, are easy to make. Three-year-old children can make beautiful little characters, but even adults enjoy creating them. The mice never look alike; one will appear to be turning its head, and another will have its head tucked down as though nibbling. A large slipper shell and two or three tiny ones, make a mother and babies. Small cowrie shells also make good mice.

Frog

Several different types of shells make excellent frogs. Green-dyed shells are usually used, but these funny creatures can be made of naturally colored shells as well.

A large jewel box (these can often be found by the hundreds in Florida, where dredging has been used in the construction of canals) or any other shell of this shape can be used. As with the mouse, the hinge is the face. Fill the cavity with glue-soaked cotton and glue on feet of small kitten's paws or other comparably shaped shells, in a splayfooted manner. Glue on big rolling eyes. Now, if you like, you may glue the frog to an inverted round shell so it appears to be crouching on a lily pad.

Another frog can be made with two cockles, one for the top and the other for the underside. Glue these together with cotton. The scalloped edge of the shell rather than the hinge forms the face, giving this type of frog a comically big mouth. Glue on kitten's paws feet to the edge of the underside with a bit of cotton and then add big rolling eyes. This frog is also cute glued to a lily pad. Paint it green or brown or use green-dyed shells.

Another frog, the most realistic of them all, is the clever little guy poling his wooden raft in Figure 7.1. The body is made of a cowrie with the toothed side at the rear. The legs and arms are augers. Glue two bivalves together with a bit of cotton to make the head, but leave the edges slightly apart as though the big, funny mouth were open. We imagine this little fellow singing as he poles his raft. Make the feet and hands of small limpets—these are remarkably like the webbed feet of a frog. Bulbous eyes complete the frog; the small stick raft made of large matchsticks and the pole add a special touch.

Rabbit

A pair of cockles glued together, hinge side to the back, form the body for a fat little rabbit, and another pair of smaller cockles, hinge side facing front, serves for the head. The arms are snail shells, the feet are two bivalves, and the ears are two smaller bivalves with the hinge side next to the head. Big dark eyes, a coil of pipe cleaner for a fluffy tail, and some bits of heavy thread or fishing line for whiskers complete the rabbit. You may dress her up with a ribbon bow, flowers or other adornments, if you like.

Swan

The swan can also be made with several types of shells. Those used most often are an olive and cockles or a single king crown.

Glue a large, white pipe cleaner or chenille wire in the open end of an olive shell. This is the body. Glue two cockles on either side of the olive with their hinges at the neck to form the wings. Now bend the pipe cleaner up into a curved neck. The swan's head, like that of the heron, is made of two coquinas, hinges up, glued with cotton to an auger or wentletrap shell. Bend the neck so that the bill points down. Either glue on rolling eyes or paint them in.

Another swan is made in quite a different manner—with one king crown shell for a body and no added wings. The points of the crown appear to be ruffled feathers. Glue the pipe cleaner neck into the opening of the shell and follow the same procedure as above for the head.

Turtle

Kids love to make turtles, and like frogs, turtles can be made using several types of shells. However, we like the one made with a limpet body, a cowrie head, and limpet or kitten's paw feet. Coquinas make good feet for very small turtles.

Glue the four feet partially underneath the body with a bit of cotton. Taper a rubber band and glue one end under the body for a tail. You may attach the cowrie head to the front edge of the body with a bit of glue-soaked cotton or make a short neck of pipe cleaner or chenille wire, gluing it under the body shell with cotton. Add rolling or painted eyes.

Penguin

For a penguin body, glue an olive point down on two coquina or kitten's paw feet. Then as always, calling into use the glue-soaked cotton, glue on a head. The head may be made of one of a number of shells, depending on the size needed. On a small penguin, a cerith works well. A periwinkle makes a good penguin head too, but you may substitute any other shell of this form, such as a brown cone shell. Glue the wings close to the body. Again, size determines the type of shell you will use: for small penguins, use coquina shells; for larger penguins, use small abalones or ivory pearl shells. Glue on rolling eyes. You may paint your penguin with black and white lacquer if you like, but we prefer the natural colors.

We would like to interject a word or two here about choosing shells for animals—you need not be restricted to those shells we have suggested; there are many more that will do, and perhaps do even better. The choice of shells depends simply on those you happen to have on hand, and our suggestions are meant merely to be examples.

Dolls

Again, as with animals, there are a number of ways to make shell dolls. They may have short or long dresses; they may be bonneted or have flowers in their hair; they may be simple or elaborate.

One of our more elaborate dolls is dressed in colonial style with a long full dress of stacked keyhole limpets. The limpets create the impression that the skirt is tiered ruffles.

To construct the colonial doll, string the limpet ruffles on a pipe cleaner. Arrange the limpets in graduated sizes with the largest at the bottom. Glue the largest one to the pipe cleaner, then string and glue the others until the smallest one is waist high. Bend the top of the pipe cleaner into a long loop and glue the end into the hole of the top limpet—this loop holds the upper body.

The upper body is made of two lucinas glued together onto the pipe cleaner loop with some cotton. At the same time, glue one pipe cleaner between the lucinas crossways for arms and glue another, curved into a loop, on which to fasten the head. If your pipe cleaners are long enough, one loop may do for both the body and head.

To make the head, glue two face shells (rounded, smooth white shells of the proper size to go with the body) together over the pipe cleaner loop using cotton for bonding. When the head is dry, make the doll's hair using tiny cup shells glued cupped side down for waves or cupped side up for curls.

Now paint on a face with eyes modestly cast down or innocently wide-open. You can glue flowers in her hair or you may give her a barnacle-beflowered bonnet. Then bend the pipe cleaner arms at the elbows and bring the ends together at waist level. Make a tiny bouquet of flowers with small gar scale leaves and glue it to her hands. Another attractive bouquet may be made of the fluted egg cases of several kinds of univalves. We have found dried out egg cases of the murex cast up on the beach, which look exactly like small bouquets. If they are too large, take them apart, clip and glue them back together in smaller bouquets. These may be dyed or painted with pearl colors.

You can make another, much simpler doll with scallops for a skirt. For a short skirt, simply glue two scallop or cockle shells together with glue-soaked cotton. At the same time glue in two pipe cleaner or chenille wire (which is usually stronger) legs leaving the upper ends to form the base on which to glue the upper body and head, as in the colonial doll above. Glue on two smaller scallops for the upper body, gluing in another pipe cleaner across for arms. These shells should, of course, be fastened with glue-soaked cotton for a bonding agent. On the upper part of the pipe cleaners, glue two face shells, and either paint on hair or use tiny rose cups, as in the doll above. Paint the face. Turn the pipe cleaner legs out ½ inch and glue coquina shells or tiny slipper shells on them for feet. When the feet are dry, glue them to the rounded side of a large shell, so that the doll will have a base on which to stand.

Now, as with the colonial doll, trim with flowers. Give her a flowered hat or bonnet and a bouquet (to hide the fact that she has no hands). However, a warning is in order: if you do not have infinite patience, don't try to make flower sprays and bouquets of this size and delicateness! They are quite time-consuming.

A long-skirted doll is made of scallop shells in the same manner, using ten rather than two shells for the skirt. The shells are lapped in tiers, with one in front and one in back and with two others lapping over these on either side. Glue on another layer a little higher up, and then a third. Forming the skirt over a paper cup holds the shells until they dry. The cup may be left in or removed later. The rest of the doll is made in the same manner as those above. You may embellish the skirt with sprays of tiny shell flowers.

There are many colonial styles of dress, but since we especially like the pretty, black-haired doll pictured in Figure 7.13, we thought it would be a good idea to give in detail the steps we took in making her.

Begin this doll by making a form out of a small paper cup (see Fig. 7.11). Cut off the bottom and pleat in the edge for a waist. Fasten the pleats firmly with a strip of Scotch® tape. Bend two pieces of chenille wire into a form for the torso and the arms. Glue two jingle shells front and back over the chenille to make the upper body. You may use a doll head purchased from a hobby shop, or you may glue together two face shells or extra-large cup shells over the upper part of the chenille neck. Paint on the face and hair.

The skirt is made in various ways depending on the shells you have on hand. When we made the doll pictured, we happened to have a few deep pink dogwood shells and some light pink ones. Taking into consideration the numbers of shells, we made a lower flounce of the deep pink; lapping and gluing the shells we went on up to the waistline with more flounces of the light pink trying to choose progressively smaller shells (see Fig. 7.12). A small ribbon sash and a flounce around the neckline finished the doll except for the trim. We made the flower decorations on our plastic work sheet and glued them to the hair and hands of the doll after they had dried.

This is the most time-consuming shell doll to make. But we think it's worth the effort (see Fig. 7.13).

Fig. 7.11 All kinds of odd things are called into play for making shell doll basic forms. For our colonial doll, we used a small paper-cup body gathered at the waist and held with Scotch® tape. The torso, neck and arms are chenille wire, and the head is a wooden ball with black floss hair.

Fig. 7.12 For the next step, add a bodice of two coral-colored jingle shells, and begin gluing on skirt flounces of dogwood shells.

Butterflies

When we find brightly colored coquina shells on the beach, looking like little spreading wings, we are immediately reminded of butterflies. Though small and delicate, this bivalve has strong hinges that hold the two sections firmly together even when dry.

Glue one of the more brilliantly colored pairs to an auger body (these can be found by the hundreds in the shelly material cast up by canal dredging). Then glue a pair of antennae to the wide end of the auger, and you have a

98

Fig. 7.13 A neck ruffle and bouquets of tiny shell flowers in her hair and hands complete the doll.

completed butterfly. We found an excellent facsimile for antennae in some artificial flower stamen, sold in bunches at hobby shops. One we especially liked had tiny oval, pearllike beads molded on the ends.

One or two of these little butterflies glued on the flowers of a bouquet adds interest. Tiny pairs of coquinas, even without the addition of body and antennae, look just like poised butterflies, when placed on shell flowers.

The same butterflies can also be used as jewelry—two small ones for earrings and a larger one for a brooch or necklace. You may also use a flower with a butterfly poised on it for a large brooch.

8

Underwater and Beach Scenes

Underwater Scene

Depicting the underwater world of the sea creatures can be a challenge, but such a scene can be constructed realistically with a little patience and study.

Start your underwater scene with a bluish green background (velure pastel paper can be bought in this color), and use your imagination from there on. One idea that works well for us is to cover the lower fourth or third of the scene with glue and to then press sand into it. Allow the glue to dry and shake off the excess sand.

Now plant colorful sea fans, sea ferns and whips in the sand. Use more glue and sand to cover up the "roots." The seashells and critters come next. Scatter them in a natural manner over the sand or glue them to the plants or on a sunken log or rock. There may be snails and a starfish climbing on the coral or the log; some limpets may cling to the sea whip.

Coral formations add tremendously to the beauty of these scenes. If you cannot collect these yourself, purchase them at shell suppliers. An hour's beachcombing on the Gulf of Mexico has often furnished everything we needed for a sea scene. But choose a spot not trampled by swarms of people.

To add even more to your underwater scene, buy a couple of small sea horses and place them upright in the sea plant trees with their tails curled in a natural posture around a limb. We have seldom found one of these little creatures washed up on the beach, though we do find many starfish, crabs and other critters.

Fig. 8.1 In searching antique shops for our oval frames, we discovered this large (18-by 24-inch) rectangular frame. It has a five inch deep shadow box. This depth made it ideal for an underwater sea scene. We painted a watery looking background, rocks, fish and sea anemones on black velure pastel paper. We then glued on dried sea horses, made a floor of real white Gulf sand, in drifts, and added a piece of driftwood. We planted the sea fan, sea whip and sea-weeds and grew some coral near the rocks. A selection of small shells and sea creatures finished the scene.

To add further to the realism of your underwater scene paint mingled blues and greens on the background. For one, we used a greyish velure paper and painted it with blues and greens and a bit of rose in rather wavy, broken lines. We like to use the soft shades of pastel paints, but oils or watercolors will do as well.

We use both flora and fauna for our plants. Though they all look like grasses and weeds, many are made up of thousands of infinitesimal animals. The sea fans, sea whips and others are in this category, and it is primarily these that we will use for our underwater scenes. Remember that if these 101 plants were actually in the water, they would be streaming out into the current of the tide, so have them do so here. We have described how this can be done in Chapter 3.

A shadow box (preferably a deeply set one) is best for these scenes. The depth of the box gives the scene the desirable three-dimensional look.

We started the shadow boxed underwater sea scene (see Figure 8.1 and Color Plates) with a painted paper background and then glued a sea fan against the background at one side. Slightly in front of this we made a grouping of sea whips with their stems planted in a bit of florist clay that had been stuck to the bottom of the shadow box (which, at this point was just unfinished board). Then we planted smaller bushes, plants, seaweeds and other sea growth at the other side. Having the largest plants at one side unbalances the scene and makes it more interesting. Now if you have some branching coral or odd sponges, such as deadman's fingers, plant these with clay.

After the planting is finished, cover the globs of clay and the entire floor of the box with an inch or more of sand (fine white sea sand is best), and you are ready to place the shells and other things to be found on the sea floor.

We laid a twisty piece of driftwood on the sand close to a planting as though the tide had lodged it there. On it is a starfish, and climbing up on the side is a crab. A clump of small barnacles and oysters is fastened to some rocks at one side. Snails are crawling on the stems of the plants, and other shells are lying about on the sand. There are, of course, the little sea horses, which are our favorites. In the foreground a small colony of tiny coquinas lies partly buried in the sand, as though feeding.

A final thought on the sea scene—when you make this scene, try to envision the sights you might encounter while scuba diving over a coral reef.

Beach Scene

Here we think dry. The background painting consists of a land scene (see Fig. 8.2). Plant sea oats and grasses, the smallest you can find, in the sand. Many of the sea creatures that were in the underwater scene will also be in this one. One difference will be that the critters will not be up in the plants. On the beach the shells lie in drifts where the edge of the waves has deposited them. They may also be piled up against a piece of driftwood or rocks.

If you are an artist, a painted background depicting a sunset in the distance makes an interesting addition to the beach scene. Paint on coconut trees, Australian pines, sea grapes and other plants you might see bordering the

Fig. 8.2 This beach scene was made in much the same manner as the underwater scene, but here we painted a background picture of a sunset, palms and plants, added a real sand beach, and planted a sea grape tree made of a sea whip and small, green fish scales. Some rocks, driftwood, shells and sea creatures completed the picture.

beach. Then plant your real plants, in perspective, as close-ups. If this scene is in a deep shadow box, pour the sand in after the larger items have been planted with a bit of florist clay. Then plant the grasses and place the shells.

In scenes for aquariums, fishbowls and brandy snifters, the above method for both underwater and beach scenes applies with the exception that the glass containers' 360° view must be taken into consideration when arranging the plants. The containers may, of course, be set against a wall, or, with an aquarium, have a background scene fastened to the back.

Try to keep the plant growth and animal life in perspective in both underwater and beach scenes. For instance, the sea oats we found growing near the ocean were too large for this small scene, so we hunted for a smaller seedy plant that resembled sea oats and used it instead.

103

9

Miniatures

Down through the ages miniatures of all sorts have been created by artists. They are among the most fascinating and valuable forms of artwork. The great artists painted miniature scenes, dainty floral arrangements and even portraits, small enough to be carried in gold lockets. Shell craftsmen too have created lovely miniature pictures and tiny, free-standing floral arrangements. Some of these are hundreds of years old and can now be found in museums.

As we gazed at our perfect tiny shells, we felt we could surely not overlook their potential, so we hit upon the miniature form to display them—but in what setting? We thought of the lovely, lacy gold frame of the mirror sitting on our dresser and immediately our minds envisioned a dainty bouquet of tiny flowers displayed in it.

So the mirror came out and we stared at the now-vacant frame with anticipation. The plain cardboard that had backed the glass would obviously not do as a background. Then too, wouldn't it be great if we could manage a deep-set picture that could be glassed over? Depth would add something special and give us the opportunity to make our picture three-dimensional.

Converting such a frame to a shadow box is not too difficult: black pastel paper is strong enough for anything so small. To make the shadow box, we cut an oval piece of velure paper to the size of the cardboard backing and then glued it to the backing. Then we cut a strip of the paper about 1¼ inches wide and long enough to encircle the oval. We fringed the side of the strip by cutting half-inch slits into it. We folded these little tabs and glued them around the back of the oval, thus forming the shadow box.

Velure paper can be purchased at art supply shops in thirty-inch sheets in many different colors. We have used this paper for the background of both large and small shell arrangements. Though it works well with medium shells, very heavy ones pull the velure finish off. This is too bad, for this paper, with its rich blues, greens, reds and black, makes a beautiful background.

The little sprays of roses in this miniature picture were made on our plastic work sheet in the same way we construct larger flowers. No cotton or base of any kind is needed—a puddle of glue is sufficient.

For the tiny completely opened flowers, pour a puddle of glue about ¼ inch across on your work sheet. Use five, ¼-inch rose cup shells, lapping each one over the other slightly as you go around. Embed the plain side in the glue with the lip side out. Then, using a pair of tweezers, drop one black seed into the center. Add another row for larger flowers, and for partly opened buds, use only three petals, cupped closer and without a center. Allow all the flowers to dry.

Now clip several pieces of fine, green-coated wire (gauge 21 or smaller) into graduated lengths for stems, the length depending on the height of your picture. With long-nosed pliers, twist a ¼-inch coil in the end of each wire and glue a flower to each.

Glue the wired flowers to the background. The stems will be anchored when the shell basket is glued on with gluey cotton. Glue some of the unwired flowers on near the stems of the wired flowers, as though growing from them. All the flowers could be done in this way, but in order to give our bouquet a more three-dimensional look, we prefer that some of the flowers stand free of the background. We also glued on leaves made of dyed sea oats (carp or other fish scales could also be used) by twisting loops in the wire at various places, but these may be glued directly to the background as well.

The miniature, five inch high, flower arrangement set deep in its ornate gold frame (see Color Plates) is the final result of our efforts.

Miniature Beach Scene

A miniature beach scene is made in exactly the same way as a larger one, but keep in mind the necessity to always have all the objects in the proper perspective as to size. A starfish, for example, might be only ¼ inch across. 105

For our background we painted a sky at sunset and some palms on gray pastel paper with pastels. You may, of course, use oils or watercolors. We then covered the space below the sky with glue and applied a heavy coating of fine, white beach sand. When dry, we shook off the excess sand, and presto—we had our beach!

The scenery must be done in three dimensions. Working from the farthest to the closest objects, we first glued on trees made of sea whips. Then we glued on shells and tiny critters as though they had been washed up on the beach. Little palm trees in high relief are an interesting addition to the background. These trees are made of green-coated wire (wrapped with brown florist tape) and gar scales, as seen in the little nativity scene pictured in Figure 6.8.

Miniature beach and underwater scenes may also be created in large oyster or scallop shells (as may bouquets of tiny shell flowers and miniature woodland scenes with animals and trees made of seagrowths). You can use marine growth of all kinds and little dried sea animals such as sea horses, crabs and starfish. This is an excellent way to display those very small things you find on the beach.

The miniatures described here are delicate and tedious work. They require great patience, but we were so enthralled while making them that it was difficult to pull ourselves away.

Shell Dangles

A little friend dreamed up the title "Shell Dangles," and we thought it quite appropriate for little three-dimensional, shell-cupped scenes (see Fig. 9.1).

Fascinated by the wide variety of tiny figurines now available in all hobby and craft shops, we purchased several sets and then tried to think of an attractive way to display them. What better way than on a shell stage with a shell backdrop!

There were sets of six angel musicians and groupings of tiny figures for nativity scenes (see Fig. 9.2). These figurines are perfectly formed. They are available in white, gold and other colors—we chose the painted figures as best suited for use with our snowy white scallops as the background.

We first drilled a small hole in the top of a scallop, for hanging, and then glued an angel musician inside the cup. The angel alone seemed incomplete, so we made small flowers of shells and fish scales and sprigs of gar scale leaves and glued them on either side of the shell stage in the foreground.

It seemed that something special was called for in the nativity scenes, so we made little palm trees, which when glued to the forepart of the shell's side seem to be standing free. The fronds of the palms, made of green-dyed gar

Fig. 9.1 Sea crabs and shells, in the talented hands of Mrs. McCree, of Matlachet, Florida, turn into delicate dangles to decorate this snowy coral tree.

Fig. 9.2 With the addition of some pretty little angels, these white scallops became Christmas dangles. The foliage is made of carp and gar scales, and the flowers of carp scales and shells.

107

scales, are very real looking. To add to the realism, we covered the wire trunks with brown florist tape.

On holding these little dangles up to the light, we got the idea of making night lights out of some of them. The section on lamps in Chapter 6 will tell you how to do this.

Pictures on Shells

Displaying photos of children in shells is only one of the many ways shells can be used for framing. Our daughter found this idea at a craft exhibit in North Carolina and made and sent us some examples. She cut down school pictures and glued them inside large oyster or scallop shells. She coated them (you may brush or spray) with a clear lacquer and then tinted the shell with pink, frosted nail polish. After the shells were dry, she bored holes in the top of each and hung them in a cluster.

Small Christmas scenes can also be framed in this way. Cutting out scenes from last year's Christmas cards and gluing them into shells is a great project for children. Three-dimensional scenes of all kinds can be made by using tiny animals or other objects in the same way as the paper scenes. You may spray the backs of the shells with glitter, but we rather liked the natural shell texture.

Place Cards, Tally Cards, Favors and Nut Cups

How about creating your own specialized place cards for your next dinner party, making them entirely of shells or of paper with shell decorations?

Undecorated cards may be purchased at hobby and craft shops, but we started from scratch with folds of velure pastel paper and made dual-purpose place and tally cards.

Cut the varicolored paper in six-inch squares and fold them. Then, cutting smaller squares of white typing paper, fold and fasten them inside the covers, book-style, by punching two holes and tying them together with gold cord.

For decoration, we first made a variety of small shell flowers with gar scale leaves on our plastic work sheet. (By the way, all of these flowers were made from a twenty-cent package ordered from Florida Supply House, Inc. and listed in their catalog as "assortment—tiny shells." I believe the price has gone up slightly, but they are still a great bargain; they can be used for centers as well. The address of this shop may be found in the list of suppliers at the back of the book.) After the shell flowers were dry, we glued them to the velure paper and painted on stems and more leaves (see Fig. 9.3).

108

Fig. 9.3 Individualized tally cards can be made from the many rich colors of velure paper you find at art supply and hobby shops. We made tiny sprays of shell flowers for these, tied a smaller, doubled sheet of white paper inside the fold, and (for permanent use) experimented with a name plate cut from a child's Magic Slate, which can be erased and used over and over (note the middle card).

If you wish, the name of the guest may be painted on the velure, but in that case the cards can only be used once. We came up with the idea of cutting small pieces from a child's Magic Slate® (which erases by lifting the outer paper) and gluing them in the form of a pot or basket to the front of the card. The card in the middle of the circle in Figure 9.3 is an example.

For other kinds of shell place cards, let your imagination run wild. For those in Figure 9.4, we simply chose a variety of shells and decorated them in the same manner as for the dangles described earlier. Then we glued each one upright on the curved side of a small cockle or some other shell that would lie flat for a base. The guest's name may be painted or inked in or attached on a small card.

One place card (or favor) design we especially liked was made of a small whelk glued with a bit of cotton to a scallop shell base and planted with a little flower made of pink rose cup shells. Another was a "pot" made of two dried sea urchins, glued together and planted with two shell flowers. However, sea urchins are quite fragile and require care in handling. Still another place card was made of a matched pair of small white scallops glued together to form a basket and fastened to a base made of a branching piece of white coral. In this basket we glued pink shell flowers. An especially easy place card or favor to make is merely a shell, such as a whelk, planted with plastic flowers.

We made some cute nut cups out of cockles, with feet of small snails to even them up. For trimming we curved a little spray of shell flowers around the rim.

Fig. 9.4 Place cards and favors can be made in a variety of interesting ways. Here are three examples—use your imagination for more.

10

Hats and Bags

In one museum in the western desert of the United States we saw a bag that was adorned with an intricate pattern of shells. It probably once hung on the chest of some Indian warrior, dangling by a thong around his neck. The bag was made of buckskin on which a pattern of small shells had been sewn. A fringe of shell beads at the lower edge was truly a work of art. When we began concentrating on shell art, the memory of the work on that bag came back to us, and of course, we had to decorate some of our own.

The shell trimming on a bag may be as complicated, or as simple, as you wish. You may start out with an evening bag or a crudely woven tote bag (we wove and decorated a very creditable bag from palm fronds), but regardless of type, when adorned with shells each becomes a work of art.

The white crocheted bag and hat in Figure 10.1 seemed to lack something, until we added the shell and yarn trimming. We made the dahlias on our plastic work sheet (see Chapter 5). We sorted out our most colorful coquinas, laying all the right-hinged shells of a certain color in one spot and all the left-hinged of that color in another pile; to make a uniform flower the hinges must all lap in the same direction.

While the gluey cotton was drying, we made the looped green yarn medallion designs. We formed them on a small daisy loom, but they would be just as attractive crocheted. We sewed the green medallions to the bag and hat

Fig. 10.1 There are endless ways to trim accessories with shells. We decorated this matching hat and bag with shell flowers backed with green-yarn daisy loops.

Fig. 10.2 A very ordinary straw bag becomes something unique when decorated with a sea scene.

112

Seeds, sea whips, sea grasses and shells went into the composition of these panels.
We glued them to black and royal blue velure paper.

The background of this large underwater sea scene is painted. The items in the foreground are real.

and then embroidered on some green stems and leaves with a large darning needle. When the flowers were dry enough, we pried them from the work sheet and glued them in the center of the yarn medallions.

Standing back and viewing our creation, we were pleased, but it seemed to need a bit more. Buds—of course! We used small, glossy cowries with two coquinas glued to the sides to achieve the effect of partly opened buds (see Color Plates).

We were happy with the basket and hat, but when we opened the storage trunk of our station wagon, the rather inexpensive straw bag we use for shell collecting confronted us. It looked embarrassingly bare of adornment, so we quickly decorated it with an entire beach scene (see Fig. 10.2).

For this type of trimming, simply gather together the materials you happen to have on hand and use your imagination. You might, for instance, start with a sea fan. Sew it to one side, and then add some sea ferns or whips. Build these background items out (the larger to the back, the smaller in front) to give a three-dimensional effect.

Now come the shells and dried animals. Arrange the shells in careless abandon on the imaginary sand. A starfish may be crawling up the basket and a sea horse fastened as though gripped by his tail to a sea fern. We noted an interesting touch in one basket decorated by a friend. Bubbles made of artificial pearls drifted up above the sea horse in graduated sizes, the larger ones at the upper end of the column. Another interesting addition was a large fake pearl glued inside the cup of an oyster shell. Sprays of sea oats and other graceful grasses and seed pods can be used to good advantage along with the shells.

Most of the sea scene material may be glued on (it holds remarkably well on the basketry), but some heavy items may require wiring. However, we found that a bit of glue-soaked cotton worked quite well (*even on rather large shells*).

During one of our safaris on an island camp, we wove several hats and large baskets. We decorated one of the hats with the wood roses of the coconut palm (the immature buds that fall in strong winds), and these were so attractive that we later embellished the design still further by combining shells with it.

This type of art is strictly original, and no one can give you step by step how-to directions for the simple reason that your own collection of shells will determine the design. We can, however, give you some idea of the way we go about planning our designs.

Actually our method is a process of trial and error, with nothing permanently attached until we are pleased with it. We get together all the items we

113

plan to use and begin laying them out on the basket or hat in various designs. When an arrangement pleases us, we begin gluing.

As to the items that may be used, we took inventory and discovered that the following have all gone into the making of our trims—sea fans, sea ferns and whips, coral, sponges, whelk egg cases, starfish, sea horses, crabs of various kinds, fake pearls, cut shells and whole shells of every type from large scallops to tiny coquinas. We have even used old, weathered rope and net corks and pieces of fisherman's net and small sections of knotty driftwood. All of these do their part in lending a flavor of the sea to the finished item.

Bear in mind, as you work, the fact that baskets and hats get rougher treatment than plaques, panels or pictures, and so their decorations must be more firmly anchored. Also make it a point not to have pointy things sticking out that will catch on clothing.

Cut shells, which may be purchased at most shellcraft shops, are excellent for trimming hats and bags. The shapes of the shell pieces are so varied, that you have the opportunity to call upon your creative senses to the utmost when arranging your designs.

The art of decorating hats and bags is one of the best shellcrafts to teach children—especially older youths who love to make items of wearing apparel. Clubs, Scouts, Campfire Girls, summer camps, vacation Bible schools, all are excellent opportunities to teach young people to express their artistic talents with shell art.

11

Shell Jewelry Making

Jewelry made of shells was by no means invented by modern man. Many thousands of years ago women, and men, went all out for shell jewelry, and shell jewelry has remained consistently popular through the ages. The lovely pearly gloss, strange forms and delicate coloring of shells have consistently appealed to man's sense of beauty. With the talent inherent in him, he formed these treasures of the sea into objects of personal adornment. Much of the shell ornamentation found in excavations was used as trimming for garments in the form of dangles, sewed bead designs, and deep fringe made of strung shells or shell beads; but jewelry, as we know it, was as popular through all recorded history as it is now, and much of it was made of shell. We know, for example, that among pre-Columbian men, more jewelry was made of shell than of any other material. Much of this was simple, small disks with holes bored through the center or cylinders cut from mother-of-pearl shell and laboriously bored with the crude tools of the age.

Archeologists finding these beads usually entitled them wampum, but in most cases this classification was erroneous. Real wampum was used for trade money and only made up a small percentage of these beads. Most were used simply for personal adornment. These items of jewelry took all the forms of present-day pieces—rings, necklaces, bracelets, hair ornaments, pendants, gorgets, and even a few, little used today, such as ear and lip plugs and nose rings.

The ancient peoples used the shells they could find in their own areas to make shell jewelry. Thus, excavations in California and neighboring states yield a great amount of abalone shell jewelry. This iridescent and colorful shell is one of the loveliest found in that area. Further inland, where semiprecious stones occur in profusion, shells and gemstones, such as turquoise and agate, were combined to make beautiful jewelry. To the south, in Mexico, early men went even further in imaginative design and used shells and gemstones in delicate settings and with filigrees of gold and copper. And in the Polynesian Islands, the trend was, and still is, to combine shells with colorful seeds.

The mundane and the esthetic uses of shells were in some cases mixed. In many cultures, shells served as money; one could carry his entire fortune around on his neck. In some countries, you might even buy a bride with a string of cowries. The system of barter included wampum among the tribes of the southwest United States. Perhaps the real value of this wampum lay in the fact that many long hours were spent in carving and grinding these beads.

But always, in almost every country, shells were used for adornment, and today is no exception. Beautiful shell jewelry is sold everywhere. It ranges in value from simply made items, sold cheaply, to elaborate inlays and daintily carved cameos.

We will not attempt to discuss individual items of jewelry at length. It is our aim only to introduce a few pieces, with step by step instructions. Then, with these basic steps mastered, you will want to use your own imagination and dream up designs of your own creation (see Fig. 11.1 and Color Plates).

You can buy small kits that contain everything needed to make one brooch or one pair of earrings. These are fine for a start and are especially good for class instruction, but don't stop there. The fun of creating involves using our individual talents, and making items of your own design brings the greatest pleasure.

Besides the shells, you need only a few basic, inexpensive supplies which can be purchased at hobby and craft shops everywhere. You will, of course, need many of the same supplies used for making larger shell items: the small electric drill for boring holes and cutting edges, cotton, glue, toothpicks and tweezers. A small vise is handy, but not a necessity.

Whole small shells as well as cut slices and pieces of brilliantly colored shell are used for jewelry. Here too you will find that fish scales are great for foliage.

You may combine the shells very effectively with other materials. For example, a shell flower, set on a filigreed disk is lovely, and brilliants such as rhinestones and other small gems make excellent centers.

Perhaps a checklist of shells and other materials generally used in the making of shell jewelry would be helpful.

Fig. 11.1 Your imagination can carry you into great creativity when it comes to dreaming up designs for shell jewelry. Almost any small shells you have can be used.

Shells

Tiny conch and whelk shells. For making dangle baskets planted with a flower, and for use as centers.

Coquinas. For little butterflies.

Small, glossy cowries. To be drilled and strung for bracelets, earrings and necklaces.

117

Small cup shells. For flower making.

Dogwood shells. For single dogwood blossom earrings and brooches and pins.

Gar scales. For leaves; when dyed red, these make excellent poinsettias.

Dyed rice shells. These make pretty daisies and centers.

Small pearl snails. For centers and lily of the valley sprays.

Squilla claws. These give jewelry an airy, sprigged look.

Other Materials

Gold or silver-colored chain. For bracelets.

Pendant chains.

Earring clips or screws.

Filigreed disks.

Small plastic or mother-of-pearl disks. For bases; in sizes ranging from ⅜ to 1 inch.

Seed pearls.

Pins for brooches.

Rhinestones.

Small gold or silver-colored rings. For attaching dangles and for joining shells.

We have used all of the above in making the pieces of jewelry pictured in this book. Instructions for making several of these pieces follows.

Earrings

For single-flower earrings, choose the smallest shells you happen to have. Decide on the kind of flowers these shells would best be suited for and then look up the directions for making those flowers in Chapter 5. Proceed as for the larger flowers. The only difference is that flowers for jewelry need a backing of some sort. We glue the flowers right on the small mother-of-pearl disks (plastic disks will do). You may also form the flower in a puddle of glue on your work sheet, and after it has dried, glue it to the disk, then glue the disk to the ear clip. We prefer the latter method.

One pair of earrings we especially like was made of two tiny conch shells drilled and hung by little rings to the earring. These formed tiny dangling baskets in which a small flower with gar-scale leaves was planted.

We designed other earrings with sprays of white squilla claws and red and white snails. Still others were made of small glossy cowries. We glued

118

bell-shaped filigreed caps to the narrow end of the cowries and dangled them with a little gold ring from the ear clip. These bell caps will bend to fit the contour of the shell, and you will find them handy for many other purposes.

Bracelets

We made a bracelet that matched the cowrie earrings described above by dangling seven gold-capped cowries on a chain in the form of a charm bracelet.

Other bracelets can be made of shell flowers glued to gold or silver disks with the filigree design extending ¼ inch or more around the flower. Fasten these disks together with little rings of the same color metal. The number of flower medallions used is a matter of choice. You can make the entire bracelet of medallions or use as few as three, with the rest of the bracelet consisting of chain.

Brooches and Necklaces

Brooches and necklaces that match the above earrings and bracelets are formed in the same way using larger shells or larger designs. You can make a flower brooch larger than its matching earrings by simply adding rows of petals to a flower of the same type, or by making a cluster or row of three flowers the same size as those used in the earrings. Glue these flowers to a disk (either the ornamental or plain type) and glue a clip or pin to the back.

Directions for making the pieces of jewelry described here are only intended to get you started. Now take it from there and create your own jewelry designs. They need not be elaborate to be beautiful. A very attractive brooch can be made of a single white mushroom coral head with three small pearls glued in a row in its center. One pair of earrings that interested us was made simply by gluing on pieces of oddly shaped, cut shells.

A mother-of-pearl pendant brought to a friend from Persia is in the more elaborate category. Both sides of this lovely pendant depict hunting scenes complete with tiny people and horses, trees and flowers. These are so delicate that they were painted with human eyelashes! Another more elaborate creation is the large shell choker necklace made of more than 200 cowrie, conch and bubble shells which we purchased in Hawaii (see Fig. 11.1).

12

Mosaics

This is a very intricate art so you should start with small patterns and work up to large ones. In other words, make a mosaic design on a small box or vase before tackling a patio table, birdbath or garden wall.

Miniature Mosaics

Our first mosaic was a really tiny one for the simple reason that when the inspiration to make a mosaic struck we were waiting for a shell shipment and had only very small shells on hand. We thus created a design only two inches wide on a crystal and gold powder box (see Fig. 12.1). A mosaic of shells this size is a very tedious project. Our powder box contained 135 shells. Some of the shells, such as the lilacs and baby whelks, were less than ⅛ inch long. Such a project requires much wielding of tweezers and a lot of patience, but it was fun and the powder box came out quite nicely.

We first drew a design that fitted in well with the gold pattern of the box lid. In this case, an eight-pointed star with inner circles looked best. In this design, we used green-dyed baby whelks and lilac shells, some purple-colored tiny snails and yellow-dyed rice shells.

We covered the inner circle with glue and placed the middle snail shell with a ring of purple snails around it. Next came a circle of yellow rice shells and a narrow ring of green-dyed welks (which look like a little wreath of leaves), and finally the star points of lilac shells.

Fig. 12.1 Mosaics take many forms, from huge to tiny. We decorated this powder box with a design of tiny shells—some of them no more than an eighth of an inch long.

121

For larger mosaics, this method is used to good effect if you do not try to work on too large an area at a time. Spread only a small area with glue, so that it will not dry before the shells are placed. The same kind of glue you use for flowers will work well on mosaics of the small or medium sizes, but grout will be needed for larger, heavier shells.

Mosaic Vases

Vases may be decorated with mosaics in the same way as the powder box above, or they may be totally covered with shells. The shells can be placed at random or in designs (see Fig. 12.2).

Mosaic Patio or Coffee Tables

The basic table used for a mosaic can be wrought iron, concrete or wood. It can be made especially for the purpose or converted by building a ½ inch high edging around the table to hold the grout.

If the table is made of wood, it should be sealed with a coating (lacquer will do). A sprinkling of coarse sand or fine gravel added before the sealer dries will bond the grout and wood together more securely.

The bonding agent here is not glue but grout. The grout can be one of several different mixtures; it may be simply commercial plaster (with this, cover only a small area at a time—it dries very quickly) or a grout made of three parts fine sand, two parts cement, and one part slaked lime, or you may even make your grout of only lime and cement.

If you like, you may color or lightly tint the grout. Grout coloring may be purchased at hobby shops. Mix only a small amount of grout at a time—it hardens quickly. If you wish to work slowly, leave out or decrease the lime. Lime is the ingredient that causes the mix to harden more quickly.

To make the above grout, mix the dry ingredients together and slowly add water, stirring well, until the mix is about the consistency of paste, or barely thick enough to hold its shape.

Spread a small amount of the mix on your previously drawn design and place the shells. In spite of the care you take, some of the grout will invariably cling to the shells where you don't want it, so while it is still wet, wipe the excess off with a wet cloth or paper towel.

You can improve the look of the crevices between the shells by smoothing them with a sharpened wooden dowel in the same way a bricklayer uses his trowel. The mortar on a tabletop should be from ⅜ to ½ inch thick for most

Fig. 12.2 These vases were all covered with a mosaic coating made of crushed shells and tiny whole shells in delicate shades of pink.

shells. If the spaces between the shells are too large to look good, fill them with fine shell fragments. You can crush shells by placing them in a strong cloth bag and pounding it with a hammer. People on the west coast will find lovely iridescent abalone shells for this wherever abalone fishermen clean their catch.

Shells of all types can be used in mosaics, but of course, it is wise to not use the fragile shells, such as tulips and paper whelks, on outdoor items. Flat bivalves, such as scallops, sunrays and cockles, work well on tabletops.

These mosaic designs may be as simple or as complicated as you wish. You may place shells at random or in carefully designed patterns consisting of graduated shells or even of flowers previously made on your work sheet. On

Fig. 12.3 Sea Grape Lodge, Ft. Myers, Florida. The walls, colonnades, arches and pillars are all embedded with giant shells. *Courtesy of Phil DeGraff*

Demere Key, an island off the coast of Florida, we came upon a remarkable example of mosaic—a large mansion completely covered with shells (see Fig. 12.3).

Another method of making mosaics is to inlay shells in liquid plastic or resin. Of course, this requires a mold. We have seen some lovely coffee tables and end tables made in this manner. The richly colored abalone is an especially good shell for this. Lay broken pieces in the mold with the most colorful side down, and pour the resin in up to the lip of the mold. If this is to be a wall hanging, partly embed a loop (a paper clip will do) in the resin before it sets. Instructions for resin casting are given in the next chapter.

13

Resin Casting

The following materials will be needed for resin casting:

Catalyst (hardener). This comes with the resin.

Unwaxed paper cups.

Molds. Pliable, plastic molds may be found in a variety of sizes and shapes, and with manipulation they will easily release the resin cast once it has hardened. Glass molds may also be used, but these must be broken to free the cast. Also, it is well to be certain that whatever mold you use does not have a rough interior; even the slightest seam can be seen on a resin cast (see Figs. 13.1 and 13.2).

All-purpose clear polyester casting resin.

Resin dyes. These may be purchased in an assortment of colors.

Plastic or wooden picnic spoons. These are used for stirring.

General Directions

For the first pour, measure the resin needed in a paper cup. Each pour should be about ¼ inch thick. Mix in dye to the desired shade with a craft stick or picnic spoon, adding a few drops at a time. Drip in the catalyst and mix, stirring for at least one minute. Now pour the mixture into the mold.

Fig. 13.1 The Mao table is graced by many lovely resin casts protecting delicate slices of chambered nautilus and other shells for all time.

Fig. 13.2 We found these colorful cast resin wall plaques at The Shell Factory. Pieces of abalone shell are embedded in the casts.

126

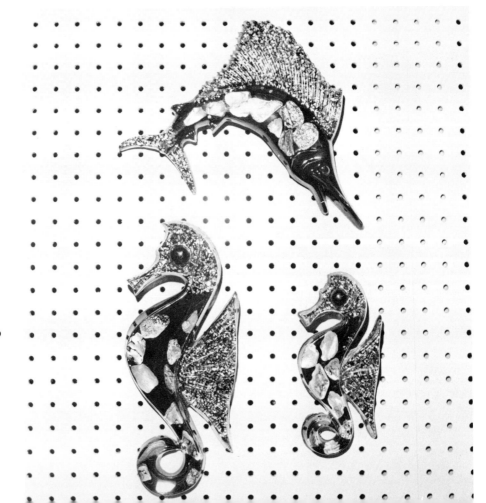

Allow this to set until the mixture is tacky. At this point the items to be embedded are added. After the items are placed, add another pour of from ¼ to ½ inch. Keep adding resin until the desired thickness is reached. Be sure the mold is standing on a level surface, and allow it to set for twenty-four hours before turning it out. The temperature of the room will make a difference in the time needed for setting. The resin sets up faster at a warm temperature.

We like to make the first pours, in which the items are embedded, of clear resin and then dye the final pour as a backing. Remember that the bottom of the mold (the first pouring) will be the top of the cast when it is finished, and place the items accordingly.

In a fairly thick casting with a number of different items, we like to attain a three-dimensional effect by placing some of the items after the first pour and others after the second or third pour, partly overlapping the first to give an illusion of death.

The amount of catalyst used depends on the thickness of the cast. As a general rule, a thick cast (one inch or more) will require four or five drops of catalyst per ounce of resin and a thin one from eight to ten drops of catalyst per ounce.

Helpful Hints

We use a measuring cup and water to determine the amount of resin it will take to make a thickness of ¼ inch in our mold. Pour water into the mold to a depth of about ¼ inch, and then pour the water into a measuring cup to determine the number of ounces. Pour the water into your paper cup and draw a line at the water level. Now you can throw out the water, dry the paper cup, and pour in resin up to the line. Don't use foam cups—the resin may dissolve them. Use a plastic breadboard or plastic sheet for a work area. Resin may damage other surfaces.

A Sea Scene in Resin

We used an eight-inch square mold for this scene (see Fig. 13.3). The first pour consisted of six ounces of resin with thirty drops of catalyst. Mix for one minute and pour in the mold. After about an hour, test for firmness with a craft stick.

When the resin has jelled place the sea horses and starfish in the desired positions (see Fig. 13.3). Then mix another six ounces of resin with twenty-   127

Fig. 13.3 To make our sea scene, we poured several layers of resin and embedded the
sea creatures in it.

Fig. 13.4 The completed sea scene in resin.

128

four drops of catalyst (use less on the second pour) and pour it over the sea horses.

After this pour has jelled, place sea whips, shells and sand dollars, and pour on another six ounces of resin mixed with twenty-four drops of catalyst. After this sets, pour a fourth level of the same mixture.

Color the fifth and final pouring with a few drops of dye (we used sea green) for a background. Allow the mold to set in a level place for about twenty-four hours, then flex the mold and turn the cast out on your plastic work sheet. The turned-out cast has a quite pleasing watery, three-dimensional look (see Fig. 13.4).

With four glass marbles glued on as feet, this cast may serve as a trivet; mounted on a varnished board, it serves as a wall plaque.

14

Dredging and
Other Ways to Collect

Dredging for shells can be rewarding, but, of course, many of the shells collected in this way will be alive. We try to avoid killing the animals as much as possible.

Your dredge can be one of many types. It can be as simple as a line dragged behind a boat for scallops. The scallop, whose tentacles are tickled as the line drags over it, becomes irritated, snaps its valves in a tenacious grip on the line and can then be reeled in.

The tangle dredge is a mass of ropes varying in length which are unraveled and tied to an iron crossbar, which is fastened in turn to a bridle and dragged slowly behind a boat. This is considered a good way to collect all species of pecten, pinna and other rough or spiny shells; the spines get tangled in the rope.

More sophisticated dredges are made of boxes, cones or scoops covered with wire mesh or cloth. These too are dragged slowly behind a boat.

You can make a glass-bottomed bucket or a box of wood with a glass bottom sealed in that will enable you to see shells under water. In making the wooden viewer, paint the sides black in order to cut down on glare and reflection.

Another way to view the bottom and spot shells is to use a rubber raft with a clear plastic window. You can float along at ease, spotting the shells and reaching down to collect them in a bag towed alongside. Use a long-handled dip net in water which is too deep for you to reach the bottom by hand. You can locate buried bivalves by their siphons, which protrude above the sand. Angel wings can be located this way, but sometimes they are so deep that they must be dug out.

Scuba diving is an excellent way to collect shells in deep water, but this is not for novices. To avoid danger you should know your equipment thoroughly and take lessons from an expert.

We collect shells from a canoe in shallow water, sometimes three or four feet deep, sometimes not over a foot. We use a long-handled net, or if the creature has dug deep into the sand, a rake with curved tines.

We have had friends who arranged with commercial netters and crab fishermen to watch for desirable shells. Wherever you see floats strung out bobbing on the waters of a saltwater bay, there are likely to be crab pots, and it might be well to talk to their owners and ask what kind of critters other than crabs they collect in those pots. Shrimpers, too, bring in a vast variety of animals. A dredging trip with one of these shrimpers can be a remarkable experience. They go out at night and must sort through the catch under a bright light as they return, keeping the shrimp and releasing an endless variety of other animals.

You may find usable shells in unexpected places. For instance, we found bleached but usable shells in sand piles that had been dredged for canals. You may scoop up coquinas at the edge of the waves along with the sand. As a wave rolls in, the little creatures appear from the sand in great colonies, then as the wave recedes, they burrow back down. You can spot large clams by their siphons. The meat is good for food, and the shells are used for such things as decorated ashtrays.

With all these suggestions for collecting live shells, our favorite way is still to simply walk along the beaches at low tide and get the empty shells. Not all, but many of these are just as lovely as the live ones. Anyway, what better excuse could one find to stroll the shores of our much-loved seas?

15

Teaching Shellcraft

Some of the most rewarding experiences life has to offer are those in which our efforts give meaning to another. Busy, interested people seldom understand boredom; they simply don't have the time to feel it. But let's face it, a multitude of people in this beautiful big world of ours are simply bored to tears. Those who have developed interests and skills that can dispel boredom should certainly share them with others.

How sad it is to walk through a nursing home, for instance, and see people sitting, dull and disinterested. Those same people come to life after being shown that, far from being useless, they can still create lovely items with their hands. We have taught ceramics, basketry, pastel painting and finally shellcraft to these and other age groups. We have watched with delight the pleasure derived, especially by the older people, as they displayed the art created by their own hands. We were, in fact, told by nurses that many of them lived in excited anticipation from class to class.

It is primarily for this reason that we decided to include a discussion on conducting a shell art class in this book. Of course, the classes can't be relegated to nursing homes alone, they can apply as well to children's groups, such as Scouts, Campfire Girls, vacation schools and camps. And don't overlook the fact that shell art of a more advanced nature is great for women's clubs and retiree groups. The classes will, of course, be conducted differently for different groups. For this reason we will first discuss methods in general and then separately for the various groups.

Many instructors have all their students make duplicate articles. The instructor stands before the class and constructs a beach scene on a board. Each student has been given a similar board and all the components for the scene (a plastic bag of sand, sea plants, some branches of coral, a piece of driftwood, a dried sea horse and a starfish). He just follows the instructor's example. This is not an especially creative way to teach art, but it is fast, and in some instances where time is short, it may have to be used.

With the above method, the instructor has all the components ready, packaged in kits. This method can also be used for flower arrangements and for shell jewelry. As we mentioned earlier, kits for jewelry can be purchased in hobby shops. A jewelry kit might contain a brooch base pin or earrings and the flower petals, centers and leaves to be glued on them. The more expensive kits contain two or three projects.

Each member of the class must be provided with either a small piece of thick plastic or a plastic-coated paper plate to work on. Each must have glue, cotton and tweezers. A tube of glue for each individual is best, but if this is not possible, then one for every two people will do. If you are using a kind of glue that doesn't wash off, be sure to have something to remove it on hand, such as nail polish remover.

It is good to have a sample of the article to be made. This holds true especially if the students are to make critters. There is quite an opportunity for creative expression with these, especially if each student is allowed to choose the components for his own. For critters you will need large and small whelks, wentletraps or augers, olives, cockles, cowries, kitten's paws, slipper shells, rose cups (for mouse ears), black seeds (for mouse eyes and nose) and some of the cute rolling eyes, pipe cleaners, cotton and glue. Spread this material out on a table along with a display of six or eight made-up critters. Let each person decide on the critter he is going to make and then choose parts for it from the piles laid out on the table.

Nursing Homes

Older people will want to make pretty things or comical animals and birds, but the instructor should choose projects that are not too intricately formed, taking into consideration that older fingers may no longer be as agile as they once were.

The larger animals and birds pictured in Chapter 7; large, free-standing flowers; and pictures with flat flower arrangements are excellent for these classes. Also good here are plaques with a variety of shells and sea creatures glued to them.

Fig. 15.1 Children can create lovely shell artwork of their own.

These classes must not be too large; individual help is required. We suggest that each instructor be responsible for not more than eight or ten students. Even with this small ratio, the work will go slowly and should not be rushed.

The main thing to consider in starting a class of any kind, is that the teacher must be well prepared in both know-how and materials.

Children's Groups

Vacation Bible Schools are held in towns everywhere each summer, and in all of these some sort of crafts is taught. Shellcraft is great for these, as

134

well as for camps and other gatherings of children (see Fig. 15.1). Critter-making is good for smaller children (from six to nine), and the more difficult items are good for junior and intermediate ages.

It is best not to try to cover too much territory in these classes; the sessions may be short, and making one or two really fine articles during the five or ten days of sessions will be best. Here too the made-up kits are practical.

Women's Clubs

With women's clubs and retiree groups, the projects can take the form of a one-afternoon session or of a long study course. The time involved determines the articles to be made. They can be as simple as a pair of earrings or as complicated as an entire free-standing bouquet—it all depends on the time and shells available. We have discovered that as a general rule these groups are made up of people who have spent some time on seashores, collecting shells. Quite often, though, their shells are of types not usable in shell art, so you will probably find it necessary to order at least some of the shells from shell shops.

There are always some who are talented and some who are all thumbs in any class, so provide both easy and difficult projects. Some class members will prefer to start with an easy project and graduate to one that is more difficult.

Ideally, an experienced instructor should conduct all classes, but since few are available, we have tried to write this book so that it may be used as a textbook for both teachers and students.

16

Collecting Areas of the World

The coastal waters of the world differ greatly in temperature, depth and other factors which determine the species of shells that may live in them. Cold water shellfish will often be of different species from those found in warm water, but this does not always hold true, for there is an over-lapping of areas. Because of this, we will attempt to list some of our own favorite collecting areas and to give the locations of some shells customarily used for crafts.

The Gulf of Mexico

We selfishly start this discussion on collecting localities with the gorgeous snow-white beaches of that section of the Gulf of Mexico which curves along Florida's shores from the Ten Thousand Islands on up north to Panama City; this is our treasure trove for shells. You may expect to find an amazing variety here, and collecting them will require several different methods.

A number of islands, peninsulas and mainland beaches provide excellent shelling. For orientation, let's start with one of the best-known islands, Sanibel. Sanibel Island, lying off the coast of the Florida peninsula, has long been considered one of the finest shell collecting areas in the United States. At one time this island was accessible only by ferry. Now Sanibel Island is so thickly populated that few of these beaches are open to wanderers. Of course, you may roam these beaches, if you can find a place to enter them, but in many places the waves have cut up into the woods and there are no connecting beaches. In spite of the heavy traffic that seems constant on the few public beaches, there are still good shells to be found on Sanibel. Here we have seen lovely calico shells and lemon yellow scallops along with other shells of this area.

One advantage of coming to this island is the fact that there are beach motels and hotels to fit most everyone's vacation budget. And if you are fortunate enough to have a boat, there are "wild" islands in this locality where the shelling is great. One of these is the island of LaCosta (or Cayo Costa) which stretches its narrow width in a long strip off the coast west of Ft. Myers, Florida, and north of Sanibel. Since LaCosta can only be reached by boat, it is still unspoiled and excellent for shelling. When you cruise to LaCosta, plan to take a lunch and spend an entire day on its shores. Remember to take mosquito repellent. The rascals rarely bother you out on the beaches where there is usually a good breeze, but when you enter the woods they will attack.

There are no motels or hotels here, but if you like to rough it, there are some crude cabins on the upper Gulf side that may be rented by the day or week. Forming a small park, these cabins have water and toilets. They are equipped with bunks, but you must bring all equipment such as bedding and cooking utensils and food. You may tent-camp here, but we would advise you to take an insectproof tent—preferably one with a sewn-in floor. We know there are snakes on the island and alligators too, but in all the years we've been going there, we have never encountered a snake, and the alligators stay in their own ponds far from the beaches.

The beauty of LaCosta's beaches lies in the fact that few people are there at any given time, though, as in all other places, the numbers are increasing. But even as late as last year, there were times during the winter months when, roaming there lost to the world, we would look up to find ourselves either completely alone or with only a couple of small, moving dots far down the beach, evidence of fellow wanderers.

On LaCosta you will find practically every type of shell the Gulf has to offer, but certain species predominate at various times and collection is never predictable. You may at one time find the beaches literally covered with brilliantly colored fighting conchs, great starfish, cockles of every size, and turkey wings; at another time the predominant shells will be scallops, clams, snails (such as the moon snails) and pen shells. This variation makes shelling here tremendously exciting; each time you land, you know for a certainty that there will be surprises in store.

LaCosta is only one of a string of long, narrow islands (from north to south—Gasparilla, LaCosta, the two Captivas and Sanibel) which curves in a 137 semicircle that stretches from below Englewood south to Ft. Myers Beach and forms numerous bays.

We roam these beaches and float on the waters of the bays in our canoe—particularly at Charlotte Harbor and Pine Island Sound. Collecting is not really good in the bay waters, but we occasionally dip up some excellent shells in our long-handled nets. We have found some especially nice large whelks, some alive but many empty and not damaged. Whelks are not easy to find because they camouflage themselves in the sand. We sometimes find shells on the small mangrove-rimmed islands lying in the bays. Only a few of these small islands have beaches, and they are circled with such a dense growth of spidery mangroves that it is impossible to land on them. But some were once occupied, and these have openings of a sort cut through the mangroves. On these we find shells, especially after exceptionally high tides or storms, which have been trapped in the roots of the trees and can be collected before they have aged and weathered. Here we have found some fairly good horse conchs and double king crowns.

Here too are the great shell mounds of the ancient Indians. Every kind of shell imaginable is found in these mounds, but of course these shells are aged and weathered beyond use. The mounds must be very old, for giant banyan and gumbo limbo trees are growing on some of them. This area is rich in history, and not only in the early history of the Indians; such pirates as Gasparilla and others entered the passes in their sailing ships to hide out in the bays from the larger, more cumbersome ships that were attempting to capture them. This string of islands affords excellent shelling.

A little farther out, within sight of LaCosta and Gasparilla, is another, rather barren island which is not named on our map. We simply call it Shell Island, for that is exactly what it is. It is made almost entirely of shells. However, as there is often rough water between LaCosta and Shell Island, it would not be wise to go out to this island in a small boat. In any case, check the weather forecasts for "small boat warnings" before going even to the string of islands—a storm can whip up in a hurry, and even the bays get rough.

Farther down the coast, at Vanderbilt Beach, Naples and Marco Island, there are excellent shelling beaches. But here again, as on Sanibel, shelling traffic is heavy. On one occasion last year, we arrived at the Naples Public Beach right after a very low tide and found some lovely deep salmon jingle shells and some rather large angel wings. The shelling along all these outer beaches is especially good after a hurricane or storm when shells will be ridged in mounds or drifts.

We have done little shelling on the strip just above Englewood and around Tampa and St. Petersburg because it is so heavily settled. But farther to the north, on the upper curve of the Gulf, there is a small peninsula (or rather an island) at Port St. Joe called St. Joseph's Point. We have found some unusual shelling here—not on the Gulf side of the island, but in the shallow bay waters. T. H. Stone Memorial Park makes up one entire end of the island. We park our trailer in one of the lots, get set up, then launch our canoe onto St. Joseph's Bay.

Last year we were in for a surprise. As we floated the shallow water of the bay, we found some of the largest whelks we have ever found anywhere (see Fig. 16.1). Some were alive, and these we left, but there were many empty shells in perfect condition with lovely, glossy coral pink linings. Many of our friends' homes are now graced with beautiful flower arrangements made from these shells. The beach on this bay is strewn with a wide variety of shells —snails, purple mussels, many hundreds of sea urchins and crab shells of all kinds and other critters that can be used in beach and underwater scenes.

Florida's Atlantic Coast

On the Atlantic coast of Florida, the shelling varies from spasmodic to poor. With the heavy surf and the heavy load of humans, it is difficult to find shells in good condition. On rare occasions we have found some fair shells which were brought in by side-sweeping waves and deposited on the outer beaches of Hutchinson Island, which stretches south from Fort Pierce. If shelling is your main interest, this is not an ideal area. However, aside from shelling, the powerful and dynamic Atlantic Ocean has a fascination that cannot be denied, and time taken from shelling for the pure joy of communing with this magnificent ocean will certainly not be time wasted. Then too, the surf fishing here is great, but the coast south from Hutchinson Island is so thickly populated that we will skip its beaches and head on down to the Keys.

The Florida Keys

This long string of islands offers a type of shelling altogether different from any we have talked of up to now. There are no wide stretches of natural sand beaches in the Keys, but there are tidal flats, and sometimes, if you don't mind a little wading, shelling here can produce good results.

We often find in the Keys those specimens of sea flora and fauna that add interest to our beach scenes and net decorations. Lying off the east coast are the living coral reefs, and often during storms, seaweeds, sea whips, sea fans, strange sponge forms and coral head are broken off and carried in to 139

Fig. 16.1 Some of the huge whelk shells we collected while wading and floating. There were hundreds in this bay. Many of them had just laid their long curls of egg sacks and others were still in the process.

become trapped beyond the high waterline in the shallow tidal pools that pit the coral of these islands. The items used in the pictures made up of grasses, seed pods and seaweeds and sea fans and whips were almost all found about a third of the way down the strip on the Atlantic side. The water in the Keys is ordinarily too hot for good shelling during the summer months; it is good in the winter and best in the springtime, when there are minus tides. Along here we often find some rather special small jewel boxes and chrysanthemum shells. We will list more of the types of shells to be found here when we discuss the Caribbean area later on.

California

As is the case in Florida, California has good shelling, if you can get to it. And here, as in Florida, there are a number of reef-protected areas that deter the pounding of the waves. In the more shallow, protected areas, you may wade out to the kelp beds and find lovely top shells, or the shells may wash up on the beaches with the kelp that breaks off during storms.

The southern shore, ordinarily affording the best shelling, is so heavily populated that going there for the specific purpose of shelling could be frustrating. Farther north, much of the coast is made up of steep, craggy rocks and wild, crazy breakers, and we have not found shelling here to our liking. Actually, along this coastal strip, we turn into rockhounds. Climbing down from the highway at such spots as the Willow Creek area, we risk life and limb to lower ourselves into Jade Cove, where we sometimes find bits of black jade, agate and red and brown jasper.

This coast can produce rare and plentiful shells, but most of the time it takes wading or digging to find them. Whole beds of purple olives can sometimes be found by digging into the sand. Turning over rocks and reaching into crevices may expose cowries and other fine shells. Be careful though—you don't want to pull your hand out with a moray eel hanging on it! Some shells here are hunted at night with a powerful light; many sea creatures are sun-shy night predators.

Some of the shells you may expect to find here are nutmeg, chiton, scallop, dogwinkle, abalone, olive, limpet, top shells, cowries, clams and cones.

Central America's West Coast

This locality, including some of the coast above (in Mexico) and below (in South America), is purportedly a rich collecting area. We have not tested 141 it ourselves, but will list some shells we have seen from here: tuns, murex, whelks, olives, nerites, cup and saucers, conchs, cowries, cones, augers, thorny oysters and wedge clams.

The Caribbean

The Caribbean waters include the Florida peninsula, the Keys, Bermuda, the east coast of Central America and the northern coast of South America. We might expect to find the following craft and collectors shells here: macoma, olives, tellins, augers, sunray venus, nutmegs, cones, quahogs, margins, cockles, lucinas, conchs, jewel boxes, miters, volutes, snails of many kinds, carditas, oysters, scallops, clams, slipper shells, whelks, mussels, tulip shells, pens, murex, figs, turkey wings, helmets, cowries, wentletraps, bonnet shells and top shells.

The Northeastern United States

We have been told by acquaintances that a good way to get the shells you want in this locality is to befriend local netters and lobster fishermen. Lobster traps in particular often attract unusual deepwater shellfish that are difficult to find otherwise. Oyster fishermen of Maryland and some New England states often find beautiful jingle shells and others fastened on oyster shells as hitchhikers. It has always seemed to me that selling shells would be a lucrative second business for netters and pot fishermen. Perhaps some do sell shells, but I have not yet found one I could buy them from. It could be that it doesn't pay enough to put in the time it would take for marketing.

There are lots of fine shells in this area. Among them are drills, limpets, snails, periwinkles, clams, sundials, tritons, murex, whelks, tulip shells, mussels, oysters, scallops and quahogs.

The Indo-Pacific

This locality covers a wide area that includes Hawaii and the Philippines. Though it is hard to determine for sure, it may be the finest of all shell collecting localities. Friends of ours believe that this area, with its many coral reefs, is one of the greatest shelling places in the world. Here again it would be great to have friends among the shellfood fishermen, who often trap in deep water and bring up strange creatures that you are not likely to find cast up on the shore or in shallow water.

It would be utterly impossible for us to cite specific spots in this area where certain shells may be found. The merging and overlapping of types of sea creatures are especially great here. But we want to give a general idea of what you might expect to find.

Here you will find unusually large cowries and unique conchs. Here too, some of the rarest of shells, the glory-of-the-sea cones, have been found. We cannot possibly name all the shells to be found here, or even all the species, but here are a few of the great variety: turritella, ceriths, limpets, nerites, periwinkles, sundials, conchs, moon snails, cowries of many types, helmets, bonnets, frog shells, tritons, murex, spindles, olives of many kinds, miters, bubbles, the volutes, augers, turrets, oysters, scallops, clams, jewel boxes, carditas, tellins and cockles.

Japan

You will find a wide variety of shells in Japan's temperate waters, though not so much area is involved here as in other regions. There will be slit shells, star shells, carrier shells, clams of many kinds (including the jackknife clam), scallops, pearl oysters, bubbles, top shells, turbans, wentletraps, moon snails, bonnets, latiaxis, volutes, turrets and cones.

Australia

Though this might have been included in our listing of the Indo-Pacific area, we prefer to take Australia separately because it is unique in itself. Like so much of her land fauna, many of Australia's sea creatures are rare species. There are, for instance, giant clams which measure three or four feet across and weigh as much as 500 pounds! The Shell Factory of Ft. Myers has several of these monsters on display, and we have seen them in other shell shops. They would be great for a birdbath, but we have not dared to price them.

Here too you will find the following, both unusual and ordinary: strange top shells, trumpet shells which are over twenty-five inches long, turbans, star shells, cowries of many kinds, helmets, baler shells, many kinds of volutes, cones, augers, carditas, spiny vase shells, a wide variety of clams and many others that are common in waters of like temperature.

143

The Mediterranean

This area includes the waters of Turkey, Egypt, Spain, Italy and North Africa. These waters contain the usual shells of the other seas of shallow depths and some rare shells as well. Here you will find helmets, scallops (the beautiful white Jacob's scallops can be found here), the purple dye murex (as well as other murex), tritons, cowries, pens, helmets, tellins and clams of many kinds.

South Africa

We are not particularly well-versed in the shells to be found in South Africa, but some of them are: conchs, turbans, limpets, cowries (the Fulton's cowrie found here is one of the rarest cowries in the world), the volutes, margins and cones.

Sources of Shells

Andre Imports, 282 Post, San Francisco, Cal. 94101
   Extensive selection of worldwide shells for collectors, decorators and artists.
Arthur Court Designs, Inc., 888 North Pt., San Francisco, Cal. 94101
   Retail.
Beach Co. Ltd., P.O. Box 190, Ft. Myers, Fla. 33902
   Wholesale only—Catalog.
H. C. Berning, Inc., 1200 N.E. 1st Ave., Miami, Fla. 33101
Blue Mussel Shell Shop, 475 Fifth Ave., South Naples, Fla. 33940
Bud's Exotic Flowers, 656 Brannan, San Francisco, Cal. 94101
   Excellent selection of decorator shells.
Col. Bill Cochran, Sea Level, N.C. 28577
   Wide selection of shells for crafts and collectors.
Diamond Novelties, Inc., 1340 N.W. 7th Ave., Miami, Fla. 33101
Edward Donav, 229 South 9th St., Philadelphia, Pa. 19104
Ferguson Marine Specialties, 617 N. Fries Wilm, Los Angeles, Cal. 90052
   Seashells, shell packs, starfish, coral—Wholesale.
Florida Supply House, P.O. Box 847, Bradenton, Fla. 33507
   Excellent variety of shells, coral, starfish and other sea creatures. Wide selection of hobby supplies, both wholesale and retail—Catalog.
Glory of the Sea, Gulf Rd., Sanibel, Fla. 33957
   Shells for crafts and collectors.

F. K. Hadley, 48 Della Ave., West Newton, Mass. 02165

Howard's House of Shells, 1234 East 14th St., Oakland, Cal. 94615

Island Hobbyland, Rt. 8, Box 280, Ft. Myers, Fla. 33901

 (One mile north of Pine Island Center, on Rt. 767, Pine Island)

Island Specimens, 320 W. Cabrillo Blvd., Santa Barbara, Cal. 93101

McCree's Shell and Craft Shop, Rt. 8, Box 50, Ft. Myers, Fla. 33901

 (Located in Matlacha, Fla.) Wide selection of hobby supplies and shells.

Miami Shellcraft Supplies, 514 N.W. 79th St., Miami, Fla. 33101

Nature's Jewel Box, Ocean Ave., The Dowd Arcade, Carmel, Cal. 93921

The Nautilus, The Dowd Arcade, P.O. Box 515, Carmel, Cal. 93921

Naylor's Seashells, 3616 Curlew, San Diego, Cal. 92101

Bus Neal, Crafts and Hobbies, 1825 St. Joseph, Mo. 64505

 Wide selection of materials and shells for crafts.

Newman's Shell Shop, Inc., P.O. Box 156, Nags Head, N.C. 27959

Royce's Shellcraft Supplies, Las Olas Blvd., Ft. Lauderdale, Fla. 33310

Sanibel Seashell Industries, Sanibel, Fla. 33957

The Sea, 525 N. Harbor, Los Angeles, Cal. 90052

Sea Gull Shell Shop, 4580 Nueces, Santa Barbara, Cal. 93110

Sea Gull Studios, Gulf Rd., Sanibel, Fla. 33957

Seashell Flower Shop, R.R. #2, South College Hill, Canton, Mo. 63435

Seashell Treasures, 715 Glover, Chula Vista, Cal. 92010

Sea Treasures, 852 5th Ave., South Naples, Fla. 33940

Shelart Hobby-craft, 263 Central Ave., St. Petersburg, Fla. 33730

The Shell Factory, P.O. Box BB, Ft. Myers, Fla. 33902

 Wide variety of shells, shell art and hobby supplies.

Shell World, 1355 Harbor Dr., San Diego, Cal. 92101

Shilling Shellcraft Supplies, Rt. 3, Box 96B, Sarasota, Fla. 33578

Southern Shellcraft Supply, Inc., 2860 Roosevelt Blvd., Clearwater, Fla. 33515

Stix Rare Shell Gallery, 13 Vandam St., New York, N.Y. 10013

Tur-Lu Shellers, P.O. Box 156, Marco Island, Goodland, Fla. 33933

 Shells, jewelry findings, cut shells and shell novelties.

146

Books for Further Reference

Abbott, R. Tucker. *Seashells of North America*. Edited by Herbert S. Zim. New York: Western Pub.

——. *Seashells of the World*. Edited by Herbert S. Zim. New York: Western Pub.

Contemporary Shellcraft. Rosemead, California: Craft Course Pub.

Cutler, Katherine N. *Creative Shellcraft*. New York: Lothrop.

Goodman, Stuart, and Goodman, Leni. *Art from Shells*. New York: Crown.

Johnstone, Kathleen Y. *Sea Treasures*. Boston: Houghton Mifflin.

Krauss, Helen A. *Shell Art*. Great Neck, New York: Hearthside.

Leeming, Joseph. *Fun with Shells*. Philadelphia: Lippincott.

Parker, Anthony. *Shellcraft*. Newton Centre, Massachusetts: Branford.

Pelosi, Frank, and Pelosi, Marjorie. *The Book of Shellcraft Instruction*. St. Petersburg, Florida: Great Outdoors Pub. Co.

Ritchie, Carson I. *Carving Shells and Cameos*. Cranbury, New Jersey: A. S. Barnes.

Van Nostrand's Standard Catalog of Shells. Edited by Robert J. Wagner and R. Tucker Abbott. New York: Van Nos Reinhold.

Index

149

Cleo Stephens is a former housewife (two children, eight grandchildren), Girl Scout leader and youth worker who describes herself as a "photojournalist-writer." In the past fifteen years she has authored ten adventure-suspense novels and over two hundred stories and articles which have appeared in such prominent magazines as *Reader's Digest, National Wildlife, American Forests* and *Camping Journal.* Dealing mostly with the outdoors, camping and ecology, her articles are adorned with outdoor scenes which Mrs. Stephens supplies from her own darkroom. Her writing credentials include the Missouri Writer's Guild award for the best fiction published in 1967 (for her novel, *The Royal Feather*).

One of only two women ever to serve as president of the Missouri Outdoor Writer's Association, Mrs. Stephens has also served as president of both the Missouri Writer's Guild and the Jefferson City Writer's Guild. She is a member of the Great Rivers Outdoor Writer's Association and the Outdoor Writer's Association of America.

Mrs. Stephens draws on personal experience in creating the local color for her novels. She and her husband, Ray, have traveled extensively throughout the United States (including Hawaii) and Mexico. Her articles reflect the conviction that the writer should possess a firsthand familiarity with the subject—the Stephens are avid fishermen and have delved rather deeply into archeology, rockhounding and shell collecting, and to a lesser degree into spelunking and scuba.